BALANCE

AT THE SPEED OF LIFE

BALANCE
AT THE SPEED OF LIFE

BARB FOLKERTS

HENSLEY
PUBLISHING

Tulsa, Oklahoma

HENSLEY
PUBLISHING

Cover artwork by Bob Elsdale, The Image Bank, Getty Images

ISBN 1-56322-088-1

BALANCE AT THE SPEED OF LIFE

ABOUT PHOTOCOPYING

ACKNOWLEDGMENTS

I have many people to thank for their love and encouragement, people who have helped to make this book a reality. My heartfelt thanks to each of you!

• To Jesus Christ, my Lord and Savior: For Your indescribable love and mercy, Your incredible power, and Your undeserved faithfulness to me, I thank You. May this book accomplish Your purposes, and may it somehow bring You the glory you deserve. You're an awesome God!

• To my husband, Dave: There's absolutely no way I could have done this without you! Thanks for all your love, help, and patience during this process, and for believing in me when I didn't believe in myself. God gave me His best when He gave me you!

• To our children: Kristi, Luke, and Anna (I told you I'd use your names in this!) You are truly our treasures. Each of you is so precious to us. Thank you for putting up with your crazy mom during this process! I'm so proud of all three of you, and I couldn't ask for more awesome kids!

• To my parents, Bob and Joyce Rae: Mom, *many women do noble things, but you surpass them all* (Proverbs 31:29). Thanks for setting a wonderful example for me to follow. We'll have to celebrate in heaven. And Dad, thanks for always insisting I use "the right word!" I love you!

• To Pastor Mark and Lynda Balmer: What a privilege it is to be under your leadership and serve alongside you at Calvary! You've made a lasting impact on our lives. Thanks so much for your wisdom, your encouragement, and your passion for God. It's contagious!

• To the folks at Hensley Publishing, particularly Christy Phillippe and Terri Kalfas, you've been a joy to work with! Thanks for all your hard work, and may God bless you as you continue to build His kingdom.

• And to all our family and friends who have cheered me on through your prayers and encouraging words: You know who you are! I couldn't have done it without you! May you reap the love you've sown in my life many times over!

CONTENTS

INTRODUCTION

Years ago, as a young mom, God stopped me dead in my tracks to show me that my life was way out of balance. Trying so hard to please everyone, I was unintentionally neglecting my husband and family. Even my time with God was often forfeited in order to squeeze in my more visible commitments. Like a Pharisee, I was trying to live the life of the Spirit in the strength of the flesh, and it just wasn't happening! (By the way, it never will, no matter how hard we may try!)

I was missing the point. God had created me simply to know Him. My time on earth was to learn how to please *Him,* not everyone else. I was supposed to be living for an audience of One, yet I was so far off track, I felt like a miserable failure. Any joy I'd once had in serving God had been replaced with the staggering weight of guilt. Where in the world had I gone wrong? Wasn't all this busyness part of being a good Christian? Was there any hope that things would ever get better? I cried for weeks, pleading for God to bring order to my life.

During those months of soul-searching, I began to dive into the Scriptures like never before, seeking answers and practical "how-to's" to bring balance into my life. The principles I discovered then have become a part of my life now. And the truths that I am passing to you in this study are the same truths that God has used to shape me. I can speak from experience and heartfelt conviction that His Word will be as true for you as it has been for me. God's Word can change your life if you let it!

Sixteen years after my feeble cries for help, I am overwhelmed by the faithfulness and enabling power of an almighty God. He has brought order and peace to my life that is nothing short of supernatural. It's not perfect by any means, but it is definitely supernatural! With three active children and a husband who is a pastor, there is never a dull moment around our house!

The difference now is that when chaos surrounds me, I've found a secret place in which I can retreat. When I slip away and come before God, I find the peace and rest I so desperately need to keep going. He brings balance to my life by reminding me of what's eternal and what's merely temporary. In His presence I find the assurance that no matter what, He is in control, and He will see me through yet another test. And that, my friend, makes all the difference!

My hope is that through this study of God's Word, you, too, will find answers and direction for your life. I've tried to be as practical as possible, and to give you a workable plan with realistic ideas to keep your walk with God balanced and fruitful.

One of my favorite scriptures is found in 2 Corinthians 4:7: *But we have this treasure in jars of clay to show that this all-surpassing power is from God and not from us.* Friends, I am simply a jar of clay — an old, cracked pot, if you will — that has linked hands with an amazing God. I have no answers for you that He hasn't already given me, no wisdom except that which comes from Him, no direction apart from His Word.

He is our treasure, and He miraculously chooses to share His life with us, strengthening us with His power for the task at hand. He is our treasure — Christ in us, our only hope of glory (see Colossians 1:27). I pray that somehow through this study, you will find Him to be your true treasure as well.

With love in Christ,

BARB

THE PROBLEM

SECTION ONE

CHAPTER 1

LIFE ON THE TREADMILL

"Come with me by yourselves to a quiet place and get some rest."
— Mark 6:31

5:00 P.M.

Quitting time at last. I leave a pile of unfinished business on my desk and race out the door. Tonight's going to be busy again, just like last night, and the night before that.

6:00 P.M.

After a quick dash to the grocery store and the babysitter's house, I rush in the door, juggling sacks and dropping junk mail on the floor. My husband, Dave, waves from behind the lawnmower and yells, "When's dinner? I'm starving!"

6:30 P.M.

After a slice of frozen pizza and a change of clothes, it's time to go. Dishes will have to wait again tonight.

"When are you going to stay home for a change?" Dave asks in frustration, as he cuts up a piece of pizza for our two-year-old daughter, Kristi. "She misses you, and I need a break!"

"We'll talk about it when I get home. I'm already late…love you!" I say as I shove the last bite in my mouth, grab my Bible, and head to the door.

Instantly little Kristi takes off toward me on a dead run, her little arms outstretched and big tears in her eyes. "Mama, Mama!" she cries. *Surely her mama wasn't going to leave her again already…*

"I've got to go," I explain, trying not to look as guilty as I feel. "Mommy will see you in the morning." And with that I have to shut the door in her face. As I get in the car, I can hear her heart-rending sobs through the open window.

"I have to go," I tell myself, holding back tears. "I'm teaching tonight, and I can't let everyone down. After all, I'm just trying to help them grow." Grow? Who was I kidding? Did I really want the women in my Bible study to follow my example?

7:05 P.M.

I rush into church, apologizing for being late and frantically trying to get organized. Putting on a polite smile, I ask, "Would someone like to pray, and we'll get started?"

Pray? Oh yeah, that's what I'd forgotten to do today. Come to think of it, it had been a long time since I'd really been in God's presence. I'd felt overwhelmed and out of control for weeks now. Always answering to everyone else first, I had practically forgotten what it was like to listen for God's direction in my life. I was tired, frustrated, and I felt far from the Lord.

I'd been gloriously saved a few years earlier, and so, like a beggar at a smorgasbord, I'd piled my plate full to overflowing with "Christian" activities. But now I was killing myself to do everything *right;* yet something was desperately *wrong.* I was just trying to make everyone happy. *Wasn't all this just part of being a good Christian? Or was it?*

Sound familiar? Share about a time when you really sought God for specific direction in your life, or a time when you didn't but wished you had. What difference did it make?

_____

_____

_____

_____

_____

_____

_____

A BALANCING ACT

As busy Christian women, many of us deal with this kind of daily commotion. Juggling schedules, children, job responsibilities, and church and community commitments while trying to maintain some element of sanity can be overwhelming and discouraging. Too often our frantic schedules keep us from seeking God's specific purpose for our lives. Before we know it, we're burned out, spiritually drained, and exhausted. What time we do take to be with our heavenly Father is reduced to one more thing on an already long "to-do" list.

Jesus' friends, Mary and Martha, found themselves in a similar pressured situation. Can you imagine? The King of kings was coming for dinner! Talk about stress! Martha's mind must have been racing: *What shall we eat? Is the house clean? All the beds made? Do I need to pick up anything else from the market? I'm sure glad Mary's here to help!*

Read Luke 10:38–42.
What were Mary and Martha's individual priorities?

_____

_____

Which of these women do you tend to be most like?

_____

When Jesus said in verse 42 that *"only one thing is needed,"* **what do you think He meant?**

_____

_____

_____

I find it ironic how these two women are remembered. The Martha Stewart of Bible days tried so hard to do good works for the Lord, but in a lot of ways, she missed it! *In her efforts to make everything perfect, she failed to see the blessing of simply spending time with Jesus.* Meanwhile, Mary's act of quiet devotion to Christ landed her an eternal place of honor in God's Word!

But in case we're tempted to look down on Martha, let's remember that she was no loser. Her resume' might have read, "Hard worker with an eye for perfection," or, "Able to adapt quickly to unforeseen circumstances." *Yet she made the mistake so many of us make on a daily basis: She became distracted by the crisis at hand and lost sight of the big picture.* Think about it. This was the opportunity of a lifetime. A personal audience with the King of kings! A Q and A with the Master of the universe! And she missed it because of housework? Ouch.

Yet how many times do we fall for similarly lame temptations and choose the temporary over the eternal? I've done it so often that I can write a book about it! Been there, done that too many times to remember, and I *don't* want to go back!

Maybe you see yourself in this picture…working so hard, yet never taking the time to be refreshed in God's presence. Maybe you're the frustrated one, constantly going the extra mile, but receiving little joy from it. *Could it be that you've somehow gotten off track, filling your time with good things without reserving time for God's very best?* It's easy to do. A frantic pace is the status quo these days, yet our loving Father patiently woos us back to a closer walk with Him.

Read Matthew 11:28–30.
To whom was Jesus speaking in verse 28?

_____

What two words describe His character?

_____

What promise does He make to those who come to Him?

_____

_____

Herein lies the reason for this study: to learn from the Master how to live life right and find rest for our weary souls in the midst of a crazy world. My goal in writing this study is to hold up the standard of who God is, and to offer the hope of all we can become as we learn to walk in His strength instead of our own. My prayer is that this study will serve as a landmark in our lives as we use the Word of God to truly take stock of where we are in our relationship to God, where we want to be, and how we can get there.

I pray that this study will challenge you to the point of change and encourage you as you discover the unmerited grace of God. In these pages I will share biblical principles that have shaped my own life, as well as practical ways to apply them. But don't be fooled! I have no "magical formulas"! There are no three steps to perfection — just hope to live a balanced life of faithfulness to God, and to your family, as you learn to abide in His strength.

And just in case you're tempted to look to me as a biblical guru of some sort, I have a confession to make. I'm just like you! Like Martha, I've lived all of my adult life in the fast lane. Our van has functioned as an office, a mobile dining room, and practically a second home. As a mother of three very active children, now ages 18, 14, and 11, I know all about crowded schedules and needing to be in two places at once. And yet, by God's grace, I am learning to become a Mary. We're on the same journey! Yet through the school of hard knocks, I am learning to treasure my time with God above all else.

And you know what? I find that when I choose to start my day with God in prayer and in His Word, I am actually able to accomplish *more* than when I don't! I used to think I had to choose one or the other — be a Mary and pray all day, or be a Martha and actually get things done. But thank God, that is not the case!

Instead, I find that through my time with God, I am directed, motivated, and empowered to accomplish all that He wants to do through me each day, and to weed out the rest. It's a win-win situation when I let Him be in control. And when I don't? I spin my wheels, trying desperately to carry out *God's* plan in *my own* strength. Take my advice: It's not worth it!

THE BENEFITS OF A LIFE OF WORSHIP

Let's look to God's instruction manual to discover the conditions and benefits of choosing to be a worshipper — living a *lifestyle* of worship that is truly honoring to God.

Read Matthew 6:5–6.
What is the condition set forth in this passage?

What is the benefit?

_____

Read Matthew 6:25–33.
What is the condition set forth in this passage?

_____

What is the benefit?

_____

Read Isaiah 40:31.
What is the condition set forth in this passage?

_____

What is the benefit?

_____

Which of these benefits sounds especially good to you during this season of your life? Explain your answer.

_____

_____

_____

CHOOSING GOD'S BEST

But this book is *not* about making excuses to turn down hard work! Serving others is a huge part of the Christian life. In fact, the two greatest commandments can be summed up as to love God and to love other people. This study is about clearing the clutter from our schedules that can cause us to miss the joy of God's plan for us. God has specific, wonderful things for you to be doing during *this* season of your life, and over the course of your entire lifetime. Don't blow them off! They're too good to miss!

Read Philippians 3:12–14.

What does verse 12 challenge us to discover along with Paul?

_____

_____

In verses 13–14, what three things did Paul determine to do to keep his walk with God focused and fruitful?

_____

_____

To really line our lives up with God's Word, we may have to drop some things from our schedules. God will most likely stretch us beyond our comfort zones at times, and we'll fail once in a while. But that's one of the amazing things about living for God: Even when we get off course, He's gracious enough to give us a fresh start each day. Thankfully, He's a God of second chances.

Read Lamentations 3:21–25.

What wonderful promise do we find in this passage to start each day?

_____

_____

List some of the characteristics of God you find in these verses, and share which one encourages you today.

_____

_____

_____

IT'S ALL ABOUT RELATIONSHIP

Maybe you've never had a "first chance" with God. Maybe this is all new to you, like a foreign language you hear others speak, but it doesn't make sense to you. I've been in your shoes — I can remember when I thought Christians were way too cheerful, and even a little strange! My lifestyle was hardly something to be proud of, and being around people who talked about God made me nervous and ashamed. I thought that if I could just avoid the subject long enough, maybe I could get through this life without having to deal with the issue. Secretly, I hoped that when my time came to face God, He would open the gates of heaven just a crack to let me squeeze in!

But then I came face to face with the Savior, and all the talk about "living for God" and "doing His will" began to make sense. It wasn't about following the rules of religion at all; it was about a very personal relationship with my heavenly Father. When I prayed to ask Jesus to be the Lord of my life, I had no idea how my life would change for the better. My heart experienced a depth of love I'd never known. The weight of my guilt was lifted, and I began to realize what all the excitement and joy was about. *Christianity wasn't a self-righteous performance after all. It was a very real relationship with the heavenly Father!*

When I made that decision, however, there was no perfect life suddenly awaiting me. Problems still came my way. But I had begun to walk hand in hand with the One who had created me — the One who had knit me together in my mother's womb, and knew my fearful heart inside and out.

Jesus hadn't come as my judge; He'd come as my Savior. If you've never met Him in this way, that same unconditional love is here for you as well. God's invitation extends across the ages to those who are hopeless and helpless, tired of trying and failing, beaten up by the world, or finding emptiness despite worldly success. God's mercies are new every morning, and they are here for you.

Read John 3:16–17.
According to these verses, what were four reasons God sent Jesus into the world?

_____

_____

_____

Verse 17 tells what Jesus didn't come to do. What was that?

_____

How would you describe God's love for you?

_____

_____

_____

Some of us come to Jesus without having gone through too much of the pain that the world holds. Others come to Him broken and beaten up from the sin that so easily entangles us. Yet we all need God, for our sin separates us from Him until it has been washed away by the blood of Christ's sacrifice. In whichever state you find yourself today, He'll take you just as you are. And that, my friend, is good news!

Read John 8:1–11.
What was Jesus' reaction to this woman as she stood before the crowds, guilty and humiliated? (See verse 11.)

_____

Do you know that His reaction is the same toward you when you truly repent?

_____

Is there an area in your life in which you have received this kind of unconditional forgiveness? If so, how did it affect you?

_____

_____

_____

YOUR LIFE HAS A PURPOSE

Is there a dream in your heart? Is there some passion somewhere down deep inside? Something you feel God wants to do through you, even if it's buried under a mountain of fatigue and frustration at the moment? Have you ever wondered if God has a special purpose for your life? Let's see what the Scriptures have to say.

Read Jeremiah 29:11–13.
List some of the promises God makes in these verses. Which ones speak to you at this point in your life?

_____

_____

_____

_____

How can we discover God's plans for our lives? How can we begin to know God this intimately? (See verse 13.)

_____

_____

_____

IS GOD STIRRING YOU TO STEP OUT IN FAITH?

Maybe you're a seasoned Christian, and lately God's been stirring your heart toward something new. You may keep thinking that someone really ought to do something about a problem or situation in your church or neighborhood — but maybe that "someone" is you! Often God will show us a need before He shows us that we're the ones He's preparing to use to fill that need! Your restlessness may be a signal that He is ready to refocus your vision or change your direction in some way. He may be preparing you to take a new step of faith. If so, relax. No matter how frightening it may seem at first, *there's no better place to be than in the center of God's will.*

The Scriptures point out two things that are — without a doubt — God's will for every Christian. Let's see what they are.

Read 1 Timothy 2:3–4 and 2 Timothy 4:5.
What two things can we learn from these passages about our purpose in life?

_____

_____

Share some ways you've incorporated the sharing of your faith into your lifestyle.

_____

_____

_____

The funny thing about God's will is that it is just that: *God's* will, not necessarily our own! Although He desires to carry out His magnificent plan through each one of us, ultimately His will is about Him, not us. As we read in 1 Timothy, *God . . . desires all men to be saved*

(NASB). That's the bottom line for God, and it will always be the bottom line in His will for our lives too.

Rick Warren, author of the best-selling book *The Purpose Driven Life,* explains:

> The purpose of your life is far greater than your own personal fulfillment, your peace of mind, or even your happiness. It's far greater than your family, your career, or even your wildest dreams and ambitions. If you want to know why you were placed on this planet, you must begin with God. You were born *by* his purpose and *for* his purpose.[1]

Read 2 Timothy 4:7–8.
As the apostle Paul neared the end of his life, he could confidently say he had finished the race. How does running a race compare to living the Christian life, and what does that tell you about God's plan for your life? What is promised to those who "finish their race"? (See verse 8.)

_____

_____

_____

_____

I believe that the key to accomplishing the purposes of God in your life is to discover the "race" God has for *you,* and then faithfully stay on course until it's finished. We must fix our eyes on *Christ,* the Author and the Finisher of our faith, not the hundreds of other things that scream for our attention. When we do, He promises to perform His work through us. Our part is to stay in our lane and keep running!

Don't worry if you don't have a clue what God's plan is for you at this point. Discovering His will is an ongoing process. He often reveals His will for us one step at a time, giving us just enough direction for the season we're in, probably because that's all we can handle! Eventually, however, just as a builder unscrolls a blueprint, God will unfold His plan before us, and with joy we suddenly understand why we're here.

The danger comes when we allow ourselves to become so overloaded with good commitments that we don't have time for God's very best! He wants to use and expand our gifts in ways we can't even imagine, to demonstrate His tremendous love to a lost and dying world. If we stay too busy with other things, we forfeit the time we need to grow in our relationship with the best Friend we will ever have. Let's face it: If time with God usually ends up last on our "to-do" list, then something is seriously "out of whack."

God loves us so much. Not because we may teach Sunday school, sing in the choir, or put a big check in the offering plate. He loves us simply because we're His: Each one of us is a priceless original. His relationship with us was worth dying for.

Read Romans 6:23 and Psalm 139:23–24.
From this passage in Romans, what do we, as sinners, deserve, and what does He offer us instead?

_____

Do you ever catch yourself trying to earn "brownie points" with God by doing good works? How might praying the prayer found in Psalm 139:23–24 help you to avoid this practice?

_____

_____

With all of these things in mind, we set out in pursuit of God's best. As we allow God to show us our hearts, we may not like what we find. But God's grace will be sufficient, for He promises that as we know the truth, that truth will set us free. We'll learn that there's really only one way to live this Christian life effectively. *Surprisingly, it has little to do with our education, our income, our talents, or our abilities.* Instead, it has *everything* to do with the following scripture passage.

Read John 15:4–5.
Can a piece of fruit grow if it becomes detached from the vine?

_____

Likewise, what is *the only way* spiritual fruit will grow in our lives? How does this relate to our walk with God and the fruit we desire to develop?

_____

_____

I want to close this chapter with a powerful little story. I include it because I believe it paints a vivid picture of God's heart for you and me, and the sacrifice He's made to have a relationship with every single person He's created.

BOUGHT WITH A PRICE

There was once a man who operated a drawbridge. His little boy, Tommy, was fascinated by the big bridge with its loud gears, and he often visited the control booth with his daddy.

One day Tommy asked his dad if he could walk along the river and throw stones in the water. With his father's permission, Tommy climbed down from the control booth and began to explore. After a while, a crowded passenger train began to near the bridge.

"Come on up here, Tommy!" his father yelled with anticipation. "You'll want to see this!" But where was Tommy? Immediately the man panicked. Louder and more urgently he called, "Tommy, where are you? There's a train coming!"

Seconds before the bridge needed to be lowered, he spotted his son. Horrified, the man saw Tommy climbing in the gears! The mechanism was so loud that the boy couldn't hear his father's shouts. What should he do? Leave the bridge up and forsake his job, knowing that hundreds of lives would be lost? Or lower it and watch his only son be crushed in its gears?

In an instant he made that anguished decision. The bridge came down. As the train passed over the bridge, he watched the passengers go by, eating and drinking merrily, without the slightest idea of the price that had just been paid to spare their lives. *He had sacrificed his beloved son so that they could live, and they didn't even notice.*

Our heavenly Father did the same thing for you and me. He allowed His only Son — His only Child — to die, that we might live. He watched in anguish as they beat Him past the point of recognition, spat on Him, mocked everything He stood for, pounded nails into His flesh, and left Him hanging there to suffocate . . . for you and for me.

The Scriptures tell us that mockers yelled, *"If you are the king of the Jews, save yourself!"* (Luke 23:37). He could have. He could have called down 10,000 angels to rescue Him, but He chose to stay on the cross. *He looked forward in history and saw you and me — our children and grandchildren. And He decided we were worth whatever it would cost to save us.* Obedient to the point of death, Jesus hung there so that we could spend eternity with Him in heaven. Such amazing grace proves His great love for us. Knowing this, do we dare spend our lives, as those people on the train, doing whatever we want? Dare we allow the busyness and distractions of life to crowd out a growing relationship with the King of kings?

Is He speaking to your heart right now? Drawing you close, He whispers, *"Come to Me, all who are weary and heavy-laden, and I will give you rest . . ."* (Matthew 11:28 NASB). Come.

PRAYER

Father, forgive me for the many times I think I'm too busy to spend time with You. I thank You for what You've done for me, and I truly desire to live as You would have me to live. Show me what's important, and what's not. Teach me what true devotion to You is all about and how to walk in it every day.

Thank You for Your amazing love. In Jesus' name. Amen.

SUMMARY POINTS

- When we get too busy, our relationship with Christ suffers.
- God wants us to choose His best over all that's good.
- Our lives are about God's purposes, not our own.
- God may be calling you to something new.

FROM PRINT TO POWER: PERSONAL APPLICATION

Your Personal Prayer Journal: I encourage you to not only answer the following personal application questions in the space below, but also use this place to record your prayers and notes from your quiet time with God. Write down your questions as well as any direction or inspiration you receive from your time with Him. As you do, you will be amazed at how much clear direction you will receive! You will also have this as a record of His guidance for future reference.

1. Circle the words which best describe your present lifestyle:

hectic	exciting	productive	apathetic
frazzled	rewarding	exhausting	on-course
focused	frustrating	growing	motivated
spinning my wheels			

2. Think back over the past week. How many days can you say you made time with God in prayer and His Word a priority? Does that line up with your overall priorities in life? If you were to multiply your response by 52 weeks in a year, does your answer gauge your stated commitment to prayer and Bible study? (That one might hurt!)

_____

_____

_____

_____

3. Are there ways you've felt the Lord prompting you to strengthen your commitment to Him lately? (For example: get up earlier in the morning to pray, set aside a regular time with Him every day, etc.) As we discussed in this lesson, list some changes that could help you grow in your walk with Christ, and then pray that He would give you the strength to make those changes.

_____

_____

_____

_____

4. When you read about something that God may be leading you to do, did something "spark" inside of you? Jot it down here. Include what it would take to accomplish it, its benefits, the spiritual significance it could have, and any obstacles that would have to be overcome for it to become a reality.

_____

_____

_____

_____

_____

5. What else do you feel God speaking to your heart?

_____

_____

_____

_____

_____

CHAPTER 2

TAKING INVENTORY: HOW ARE YOU DOING?

"Search me, O God, and know my heart . . ."

— Psalm 139:23

Years ago when I began to realize that my life was seriously out of balance, I began reading every kind of Christian self-help book I could get my hands on, hoping to find answers and direction for the needed changes in my life. To my disappointment, most of what I found was a whole lot of "don'ts:" "Don't do this," "Don't do that." It was all so negative, and much of it gave conflicting opinions. After several months of this kind of study, I was more confused than I had been when I started!

I remember asking the Lord about it one day: "If I'm *not* supposed to do all this stuff, then what am I *supposed* to do?" With that, His gentle direction came to my heart: "Study Proverbs 31." I followed His directive and found that in a mere twenty-two verses God had outlined His plan for women — of any time and culture. Proverbs 31 is guaranteed to be the simplest — yet the most challenging — list of "dos" you will ever lay your eyes on! I had found my answer — the problem suddenly became how to live it out.

When you experience difficult situations, are you more likely to first seek answers through friends, books and magazines, or the Bible?

_____

Have you ever experienced a situation in which you received so much conflicting information about what to do that you became confused about what God wanted you to do? Explain. How was the situation resolved?

_____

_____

_____

Read Proverbs 31:10–31.

Get your pencils ready! It's time to see how we measure up against God's "model woman!" The following inventory contains a list of true or false questions designed to help you gauge where your priorities lie and where you might need to work on finding balance. I have attempted to adapt Proverbs 31, verse by verse, to the modern American lifestyle so that we can see how it still applies today. You will notice that many of these verses not only address very practical elements of womanhood, but they have a spiritual application as well.

Many of the questions on this test refer to a woman's marriage and/or family life. If you're single, with or without children, answer these particular questions with your closest loved ones in mind. The scoring will work out the same.

Are you ready? Let's begin.

HOW DO YOU MEASURE UP?

SELF-TEST: Check the answer that best describes your daily routine. Be honest!

Verse 10:

1. I try to live so that my integrity and character will bless my husband instead of hinder him. O TRUE O FALSE

2. I realize that I am valuable to God, and to others. O TRUE O FALSE

Verse 11:

3. I do my best to be trustworthy, and I don't hide things from my husband even if I know they will upset him. O TRUE O FALSE

Verse 12:

4. Being kind to my husband is a daily priority in my life, and I do my best to honor him. O TRUE O FALSE

Verse 13:

5. I am a hard worker. ○ TRUE ○ FALSE

6. I don't harbor resentment about my responsibilities to my family; instead, I try to keep a positive attitude, always eager to make an investment into their lives. ○ TRUE ○ FALSE

Verse 14:

7. My family's cupboards and refrigerator are adequately stocked to meet our needs, and I try to maintain a well-organized home. ○ TRUE ○ FALSE

Verse 15:

8. I make certain that my family is well fed, always keeping good nutrition in mind. ○ TRUE ○ FALSE

9. I nourish my children with "spiritual food" as well, providing them with generous helpings of God's love and His Word on a regular basis. ○ TRUE ○ FALSE

Verse 16:

10. I spend my family's money wisely. Instead of being an impulsive buyer, I invest in things that will benefit my family, and I try to be a good steward of all the resources God has entrusted to me. ○ TRUE ○ FALSE

11. I "plant" the truths that God has taught me into the lives of others, knowing that if I sow to the Spirit in them, we will both reap a harvest. ○ TRUE ○ FALSE

Verse 17:

12. I am determined to "stay in shape" physically as a testimony of God's power in my life. ○ TRUE ○ FALSE

13. I am determined to "stay in shape" spiritually as a testimony of God's power in my life. ○ TRUE ○ FALSE

Verse 18:

14. I feel good about my accomplishments and about the investment I'm making into the lives of my family and others. ○ TRUE ○ FALSE

15. Even when I'm tired, I'm willing to stay up late or get up early if someone in my family needs me, realizing that God will bless me as I serve them. ○ TRUE ○ FALSE

Verse 19:

16. I use my skills and talents to benefit my family, and I never try to avoid hard work. ○ TRUE ○ FALSE

17. I don't avoid spiritual "hard work" either, always diligently praying for God's will in our lives and doing my best to help each member of my family grow in their walk with God. ○ TRUE ○ FALSE

Verse 20:

18. When I sense the Lord prompting me to lend a helping hand to someone in need, or to open my arms to them in love, I do my best to help them. ○ TRUE ○ FALSE

19. I extend my life to those around me who are spiritually "needy" as well, gently sharing my faith with them as the Spirit leads me. ○ TRUE ○ FALSE

Verse 21:

20. My family is almost always adequately prepared with appropriate clothing that is clean and in good repair, from mittens to swimsuits. ○ TRUE ○ FALSE

21. During hard times, I do my best to trust in God, knowing that I've covered myself and each member of my family in prayer, and that we're all covered by the blood of Jesus. ○ TRUE ○ FALSE

Verse 22:

22. I always try to take the time to dress neatly and make myself presentable, knowing that I'm Christ's ambassador wherever I go. ○ TRUE ○ FALSE

23. I understand that I'm "clothed" in the righteousness of Christ through His blood that was shed for me at Calvary. Although I'm not perfect, I have been adopted into God's family, my sins have been washed away, and I'm confident of Christ's redemptive work in me. ○ TRUE ○ FALSE

Verse 23:

24. I refrain from speaking negatively about my husband behind his back, or doing anything else that could hurt his reputation with his peers. Instead I always try to be the kind of best friend and wife that makes him proud. ○ TRUE ○ FALSE

Verse 24:

25. I use my talents and skills to benefit my family, both financially and in maintaining an organized household. I am both diligent and industrious. ○ TRUE ○ FALSE

Verse 25:

26. I know who I am in Christ, and I try to live daily in His strength.   ◯ TRUE   ◯ FALSE

27. For the most part, I'm not a worrier because I've learned that my family and I are in God's hands. That gives me God's peace, and inspires me to do all I can to prepare my family for all the good things God has in store for them.   ◯ TRUE   ◯ FALSE

Verse 26:

28. I make a genuine effort to watch my words, making sure they are only kind, true, and pleasing to God.   ◯ TRUE   ◯ FALSE

29. I try to faithfully pass on the wisdom and counsel I receive from God's Word to those around me, and especially to my children.   ◯ TRUE   ◯ FALSE

Verse 27:

30. Most of the time, our house is clean and orderly, and the details of my family's lives are organized and under control.   ◯ TRUE   ◯ FALSE

31. I do my best to stay alert to the prayer needs of my family members, and I go to God daily on each one's behalf.   ◯ TRUE   ◯ FALSE

Verse 28:

32. I try to live a life that is worthy of my family's respect and appreciation.
◯ TRUE   ◯ FALSE

33. Those who are watching my Christian life can see the fruit of kindness in our family as I treat my children with loving care and they treat me with respect.   ◯ TRUE   ◯ FALSE

Verse 29:

34. I feel good about the example I'm setting as a Christian woman and/or wife and mother through God's strength.   ◯ TRUE   ◯ FALSE

Verse 30:

35. I truly believe that any honor that comes my way is because of God's work in my life. As I focus on Him rather than on worldly gain, I give Him all the glory   ◯ TRUE   ◯ FALSE

Verse 31:

36. I believe that I will reap what I sow in everything that I do. Therefore, I daily lay down my life for Christ, trusting that my works and my lifestyle will speak well of me.
◯ TRUE   ◯ FALSE

SCORING: Count how many times you answered "true," and look below for your score.

9 or less: You're headed in the right direction! Maybe this study will inspire you to take another look at God's "instruction manual."

_10–18:_ You're moving forward! Keep up the good work, and allow God to keep molding you into His image!

_19–27:_ Great job! Your efforts are paying off, but there are probably still a few areas on which you need to work.

_28–36:_ Wow! You're being changed into the image of Christ as you allow Him to work in your life. Continue to _let your light so shine before men,_ [in such a way] _that they may see your good works, and glorify your Father which is in heaven"_ (Matthew 5:16 KJV). Keep your eyes on Christ and give Him all the glory!

Summarize the basic priorities of the Proverbs 31 woman.

_____

_____

How do all of this woman's more "practical" attributes (her business sense, her concern for her family's food and clothing) relate to her godliness?

_____

_____

On which areas from the survey do you need to work? What might you do to become more like the Proverbs 31 woman in these areas?

_____

_____

_____

EASILY DISTRACTED

Keeping God first in our lives takes diligent effort. Too often we allow the distractions of life to squeeze out our precious time with God. But without His strength and direction, our works will become an end in themselves, done more often to please man than to please God. Gradually we experience less and less of the power of God, and instead find ourselves attempting to do the work of the Spirit in the power of the flesh. It doesn't work! *When we try to live godly lives in our own strength, our energy fades, our focus blurs, and life becomes burdensome.*

When our calendars are crammed to the breaking point with things that God hasn't intended for us to do (even if they are "good" or "spiritual" things), we become distracted from the true and awesome purposes He has for us. Instead of pursuing those things, we allow our time to be eaten up by all kinds of other meaningless, or "urgent," commitments.

Although our intentions are good, we are lured onto that treadmill of overcommitment like a child is lured by the promise of candy. And then we wonder why we have turned into the Wicked Witch of the West! It's because we haven't had enough sleep or enough time to become refreshed and get refocused in God's presence. It doesn't take long until our spouses, families, and even God Himself are left in the dust, while we desperately try to stay on top of it all. Been there? In the Land of Distractions and Overwork, I've reigned as queen — and it wasn't pretty!

Read Matthew 7:21–23.

What do you suppose Jesus' disciples thought of His words in this passage? What might they have thought about the people spoken of in verse 22?

_____

_____

What two things did Jesus say they had overlooked, even with all their zeal? (See verses 21 and 23.)

_____

_____

How do Jesus' words challenge you with regard to setting priorities in your life?

_____

_____

Diversion can be a great enemy to Christians. As frequently as we get talked into taking on too much, we also get talked out of doing more important things that we know we should do.

Read Matthew 7:24–27.

What are the two key actions listed in verse 24 that will make a person wise?

_____

_____

Has there ever been a time when you knew God's direction for your life but didn't act on it, or a time when you acted impulsively without praying about it first? What was the result?

_____

_____

_____

_____

Another signal that we have become distracted from God's plan is a subtle resentment that begins to grow in us toward others whom we feel aren't "pulling their load." Granted, there are "spectators" in every church. Yet if we find ourselves harboring bitter feelings against them — or anyone else, such as our husband or children — we'd better check our motives. Bitterness will eat us alive if we let it.

If we allow ourselves to become obsessed with who's *not* doing what, we will become negative and critical, and the joy of the Lord will disappear in a heartbeat. Let's not waste our time hounding them and browbeating them in frustration! The Holy Spirit will work on them; we have enough to do just keeping our own hearts right.

When we fail to save time for the most precious people and priorities in our lives, and instead say yes to a hundred and one less important needs, life becomes messy, disorganized, and stressful real fast. An evening here, an afternoon there, and before we know it, we've squandered the time God gave us to nurture our families and make our own special contribution to His kingdom. Rather than being *driven by need,* we need to be *directed by the Spirit.*

Let's see what the Bible says about meeting everyone else's needs while neglecting those of our family.

Write out 1 Timothy 5:8.

_____

_____

What oversight is listed in this verse? What two things does God say about it?

_____

_____

What message does it send to our closest loved ones when we neglect to provide for them — whether physically, emotionally, or spiritually?

_____

_____

Are there any needs you've been neglecting in your own family? If so, what can you do to change the situation?

_____

_____

In the Greek language, the word _provide_ is taken from two words that mean "to think about, to regard, to understand or respect ahead of, in front of, or prior to."[1] In other words, _we have been instructed to think of — and respect — the needs of our immediate families ahead of, or prior to, those outside of our households._ Our family members, those in our households, take top priority, closely followed by those in the body of Christ.

So what happens when we don't make our families our priority? God's Word says that we're worse than unbelievers! Why might that be? Because we come across so hypocritical! We get so busy saving the world that the basic needs of our own flesh and blood are neglected. Ouch!

Fortunately, however, 1 Timothy 5:8 doesn't have to be a negative verse. It can actually provide us with positive steps that we can take, and it does this in three ways:

1. With few exceptions, this verse provides a black-and-white principle that we can use to direct our daily choices and keep us in sync with God's will. We can literally sit down with our Daytimers and plan our days and weeks according to this verse. That's helpful!

2. This verse motivates us to make our families a priority in our lives — and our families will know that their wife, mom, daughter, sister, or whoever loves them, because we will have taken the time to focus on their needs.

3. This verse motivates us to share our love in tangible ways, and this can go a long way toward winning our lost relatives to Christ. As I treat them with the same love that I have for my brothers and sisters in Christ, God's love in me can build a bridge to their salvation. Let's never forget that!

If I had a bullhorn, I'd use it to announce this next sentence: *Serving others is a huge part of serving God!* Jesus said that He came not to be served, but to serve. He modeled the life of a servant throughout His time on earth. *Yet just as God doesn't want us to neglect our families in order to reach the world, neither should we neglect the world to "worship" our families!* One way to avoid this is to allow our children to serve, to work in ministry, alongside of us. By doing this, we model a servant lifestyle to them, and spend time with them at the same time!

THE KEY TO OVERCOMING DISTRACTIONS

The key to overcoming distractions is to serve *when* and *where* God directs us, so that our service brings forth as much lasting fruit in God's kingdom as possible. It also involves knowing when to say "no," so that more important things aren't overlooked at home while we're out trying to save the world. God's custom-designed plan for us always takes into consideration our workload and responsibilities, and He supplies the time and resources we need to accomplish the things He would have us to accomplish. But it only works when we do it His way. This often requires that we learn to say "no" to man once in a while, and say "yes" more often to the Spirit of God.

Read Revelation 2:2–5.
God's priorities are revealed in these verses. From this passage, what can you see is most important to God?

_____

_____

Verse 5 lists three practical ways to implement these priorities in our own lives. What are these ways, and how are they relevant to us today?

_____

_____

_____

At times I've wondered how Jesus managed to meet all the needs that He saw around Him. Often He'd minister all day long and late into the evening, only to have a crowd waiting for Him again in the morning when He woke up! He was surrounded with needy people, as we are, and yet He had a secret for determining what to do and what not to do. *If we could only learn this secret, it could change our lives!*

Read Mark 1:32–38.
List some of the demands that were on Jesus in this passage.

_____

_____

What was His dilemma that morning, and how did He decide which opportunity for ministry was most important?

_____

_____

How did His quiet time with the Father help Him that day?

_____

How could Jesus' model encourage you in dealing with all the demands that are made on your time?

_____

_____

_____

It all comes down to this: *When we decide to no longer allow distractions to dictate what we do, and instead we seek God's direction in all of our commitments, our lives gradually become blessed, focused, and fruitful.* But when we don't, the elusive dreams we chase are disappointing at best, disastrous at worst.

Read Ephesians 5:15–17 and Galatians 6:7–9.

In the Ephesians passage, what three things does God call us to do?

_____

Why is the last part of Ephesians 5:17 so important, and how could it help us to stay focused?

_____

_____

According to the Galatians passage, how can we practically "sow to the Spirit," and what promise are we given if we do? (See especially verse 9.)

_____

_____

ONE SHOT AT THIS LIFE

If there's one thing that has become crystal clear to me over the years, it's this: I have only one shot at this life, and I want to give it my all! I have one shot to raise my kids to become godly adults. I have one shot to be a great wife and mother, daughter, sister, and friend. I have one shot to reach those around me with the Good News of Jesus Christ. But above all, _I have one shot to accomplish God's purpose for my life, and all of eternity to enjoy the blessings if I do!_ So, no matter what, I'm going for it!

Author Rick Warren writes:

> God was thinking of you long before you ever thought about him. His purpose for your life predates your conception. He planned it before you existed, _without your input!_ You may choose your career, your spouse, your hobbies, and many other parts of your life, but you don't get to choose your purpose. The purpose of your life fits into a much larger, cosmic purpose that God has designed for eternity."[2]

We're part of a plan that's much bigger than us! Every hour we have on this earth is a gift from God, and an opportunity to be used by Him to fulfill His purposes. Friends, we don't have to wander through life aimlessly searching for the next thrill to experience or the next trinket to buy. We can live with purpose and direction when we're on a mission for God — a "Mission *Possible!*"

Read Jeremiah 29:11–13.

What five things does God promise in these verses? Do you believe they are true for *you*?

_____

_____

_____

What is the one thing that you would regret if you *don't* do it in your lifetime? What's preventing you from doing it?

_____

_____

_____

The first time I discovered this passage from Jeremiah, it was during one of the lowest points in my life. My circumstances had convinced me that I had no future and no hope. I wrestled with the lie that if I truly trusted God with my whole heart, things would only get worse, and my life would become lonely and boring.

How far from the truth! God's Word is true, for you and for me. He has a *wonderful* future and a hope for each of us, which will be realized as we willingly hand Him the reins of our lives. Since that day twenty years ago when I decided to trust God with my future and my hopes, my life has radically changed for the better. I've been blessed beyond my wildest dreams with a wonderful husband, family, and ministry. *God has turned my life around as I follow Him daily, and He longs to do the same for you!*

But this will never happen if we sit on the fence! We can choose to be spectators in this thing we call Christianity, or we can get in the game, step onto the court, and contribute to the team. One choice is safe and boring; the other is risky and exhilarating! Although we may make mistakes, our loving Father is able to pick us up and set us back on our feet again. And as the saying goes, the only true failure is the one who never tries. How sad it would be to get to heaven and realize all the exciting things God had for us that we missed!

THE FEAR FACTOR

Why don't more people go after God's plan for their lives with their whole hearts? Why aren't there more Christians serving God with the same intensity as the disciples did in the Bible? Some are, but for those who haven't yet plugged into God's plan for them, there seem to be at least two common denominators. Let's see what the Scriptures have to say about them.

Read Deuteronomy 1:19–36.
According to the last part of verse 21, what two things were causing the Israelites to hold back?

_____

_____

Has there ever been something you felt God wanted you to do, but you allowed fear or discouragement to stop you? Or, has there ever been a time when you conquered your fear or discouragement through God's strength, and were able to accomplish something far beyond your abilities? Share the results of either experience.

_____

_____

_____

_____

_____

We can learn many different lessons from these verses. God was telling His children that it was time to step out in faith and "possess the land" He had promised to give them. But even if it was their promised inheritance, it would still require courage and great effort on their part to see it come to pass. So often God wants to move us into something new and exciting, but we quit too early! We get scared, overwhelmed, or discouraged, and so we decide to take our ball and go home!

Fear and discouragement are two of Satan's most effective weapons against Christians. Fear tells us, "Don't go there — it's dangerous, and you might get hurt!" Discouragement whispers, "You're not strong enough; it will never happen; you don't have what it takes;

you're the wrong person; you'd better give up now before you fail!" Haven't we all heard these thoughts echoed in our own minds over the years? We muster up our courage and agree to tackle something new, only to find that fear and discouragement are waiting in the wings, ready to ambush our faith.

Yet as we choose to trust God, *He* will accomplish *His* work *through us.* When we've heard from God, we can give Him our fears and discouragement, minute by minute if necessary, and then trust Him to do His work. He is able!

Read 2 Corinthians 12:9–10.

What three things can we learn about our weaknesses from this passage? If these are true, how does that challenge your thinking about the things God may call you to do?

_____

_____

_____

REMAINING FOCUSED AND FAITHFUL

Every day we face new challenges designed by our enemy to frighten us away from God's plan, or to keep us so busy that we never have time to do what God wants us to do. *The way to overcome these challenges is to remain focused and faithful!* I know that's easier said than done, but those who make this daily choice will reap the rewards for their diligence. Put it this way: We all have been given twenty-four hours in each day. How we choose to use them will make the difference between fulfilling God's plan and missing His will for our lives. God probably won't call us to part the Red Sea any time soon, or to kill any giants over our lunch hour! But He *will* call us to be faithful rather than fearful.

Let's see what the Word says about this kind of faithfulness.

Read Matthew 25:14–29.

What can we learn from these verses about the rewards of being faithful, as opposed to being fearful? How can being faithful in the small things help us stay focused on what God wants us to do in the long run?

_____

_____

_____

_____

As women, we're called to be faithful in the "small things" at home first — helping our kids with their homework, fixing dinner, adjusting or postponing our careers to meet our children's needs, even handling our money wisely when the sale ads beckon us to shop 'til we drop! We're called to be faithful to continue praying for that prodigal son or daughter when all hope is lost, to overcome addictions and the enemy's strongholds through prayer, and to believe that God's Word is true for us even when our circumstances look bleak.

God also calls us to be faithful to *follow.* God didn't expect Moses to lead over a million people in the world's largest relocation plan all on his own! Just like us, Moses, too, was called to simply follow God, to listen for God's every word and then to faithfully obey Him, whether he understood God's reasoning or not. Moses simply followed God . . . while a million or so people followed him! No pressure!

Most of all, God calls us to be faithful in our time with Him. We simply *must* take the time to wait on Him for our direction *each day,* and build that intimate relationship with Him that will give us joy and purpose in our lives. As busy wives and moms in today's world, this is the only way we can stay focused and faithful to God's Word.

But what do we do when God asks us to join Him in doing something that's way out of our league? That's when we need to be *especially* faithful in our study of the Word and in prayer, in keeping our households in order, and in remaining unhindered by unorganized or over-indulgent lifestyles. Then, as we faithfully stand on His promises, God will do His work through us!

LIVE THE ADVENTURE!

The good news is that God will never call us to do anything in our *own* strength or ability. The bad news is He *will* call us to do many things *beyond* our own strength and abilities so that we will learn to walk by faith and not by sight! That may seem like bad news — but it really is the *best* news! We have a loving Father, the Creator of the universe, who loves us enough to trust us to take part in His supernatural work. He loves us enough to allow us to endure tests and trials, knowing they will teach us perseverance until, as it says in James, we are *mature and complete, not lacking anything* (1:4). That's real love.

Serving God and walking by faith can be the adventure of a lifetime! Like a fairy tale come true, by faith we can slay fiery dragons and conquer fierce enemies — by faith we help set people free and will ride off in victory with the Prince of peace!

Dear friend, don't ever settle for less than God's best. Life is too short! How boring it is to get caught up in the distractions of the world when we can be on the cutting edge of what the King of kings is doing! Instead, abandon yourself to the will of God, for as Matthew 16:25 tells us, *whoever loses his life for me will find it.* You'll never regret it. Life is meant to be an adventure in faith! You can trust God with every detail of your life. I have, and I have never regretted it! Won't you do the same?

PRAYER

Father, I want so much to be in the center of Your will, to live according to Your purposes. I want to live above distractions, to say "no" to things that aren't a part of Your plan for me and "yes" to the things that are. I want to honor my family the way You want me to, to be in the game and not to just sit back and watch others play. I dedicate myself to listen for Your voice this week. Teach me, Lord, what it means to be wholly devoted to You. In Jesus' name. Amen.

SUMMARY POINTS

• God's timeless plan for women can be found in Proverbs 31.
• The key to overcoming distractions is to serve *when* and *where* God directs us.
• We get one shot at this life to influence others and fulfill God's purposes.
• God invites us to live the adventure as we become focused and fruitful.

FROM PRINT TO POWER: PERSONAL APPLICATION

1. Spend a few minutes reviewing the self-test on pages 30–34. List the verses that challenged you, making note of your strengths or weaknesses in these areas.

_____

_____

_____

_____

2. Next, ask God to reveal His "strategy" for you to make strides in several of those areas. List some specific ways you can work on them over the next few weeks. Here are some examples of what I mean:

A. **PROBLEM:** (verse 12) No intimate time with my husband.

PLAN: Make arrangements with a friend or neighbor to trade childcare for an evening. Then surprise my hubby with his favorite dinner by candlelight and a romantic evening! (This can be done on a shoestring budget, and it can go a long way toward rekindling intimacy in your marriage.)

B. **PROBLEM:** (verse 22) I feel fat and ugly; my clothes are outdated, and the only thing tighter than my favorite jeans is my budget!

PLAN: 1. I will choose a healthy eating plan, and begin to walk or jog daily.
2. I will take advantage of a free facial, or splurge for a new hairstyle to update my look.
3. I will give my wardrobe an overhaul. I will give away those "treasures" that are either outdated or are no longer flattering, mend what needs to be mended, polish shoes, etc. Then I'll hit the discount stores for those few things that can pull together some new outfits. (You'll look and feel better soon!)

3. Take a moment to think about how you honestly feel about yourself. Are you on track with God? Do you know Him as a personal friend, or do you see Him as a character from ancient history? Do you believe He loves and understands you, that He knows your needs and cares about your future? Are you "in the game" or are

you watching from the bench? Pray about these things, and then write your thoughts and feelings here.

_____

_____

_____

_____

_____

_____

_____

_____

_____

_____

_____

CHAPTER 3

OUR DISTRACTIONS AFFECT OTHERS

"Do not be deceived: God cannot be mocked. A man reaps what he sows."

— Galatians 6:7

Each of us has tossed a stone into a pond and watched the ripples spread across the water. Just as the impact of that one tiny pebble expands to affect a much larger area of the pond, our lives are leaving imprints in the lives of more people than we could ever imagine. That means that whether we're living in constant chaos, or abiding in the peace of Christ amid life's circumstances, someone is always watching our actions and reactions.

That can be a scary thought, especially for moms! So many of us live life in the fast lane, trying to be everything for everyone. Obviously some late nights and taxi service runs are included in our job description! But when we allow our excessive commitments to steal our joy or our time with God, or when they prevent us from meeting the needs of our families, everyone feels it. As the saying goes, "If Mama ain't happy, ain't nobody happy!" Our family knows that that's true — just ask my kids! (On second thought, don't!)

How do you relate to the "ripple-in-the-pond" analogy?

_____

_____

What's the biggest stress-producing factor at your house? Are there any ways to relieve the stress associated with this problem?

_____

_____

_____

_____

_____

Life often keeps throwing juggling balls to women from every direction. Some of that juggling is actually God's work in us, as He stretches us to *do* more and *be* more than we could ever do and be without His strength. That's a good thing! When we reach out to others in response to God's leading, we come away with the satisfaction and peace of knowing we have pleased our heavenly Father.

But then there are those times when we are manipulated into attending another meaningless social event, knowing full well that God would rather have us spend that time with Him or with our families. We think we can just suck it up and forfeit a little sleep to get everything done, but in reality, our stress and fatigue affects everybody around us.

Who hasn't experienced that awful feeling of making time for everyone else's needs except for those under our own roof? We end up frustrated and exhausted, wishing we had never said yes to the party, to the fund-raiser, to whatever it is that keeps us away from what we should be doing. And what is the source of this frustration? *It is the fact that we chose to please man rather than please God.*

Read Galatians 1:10.

When we're faced with so many options, how do we decide which are the most important?

_____

_____

To whom do we ultimately answer, and how could remembering this fact help us as we go about our daily lives?

_____

_____

WHO PAYS THE PRICE WHEN WE OVERCOMMIT OURSELVES?

1. OVERCOMMITMENT AFFECTS OUR RELATIONSHIP WITH GOD.

You may rationalize, "But I do so many spiritual things!" How easily we can become fooled into thinking our efforts to *do* things for God can ever replace the benefits of just *knowing* Him. Maybe if we were to receive an engraved invitation that said, "The King of kings requests your presence," we'd be more likely to pencil Him into our schedules! He longs to have an intimate relationship with us, to shower us with His love, to direct our lives for our good and His purposes. It's an opportunity that's too good to miss!

Read Luke 15:11–24.
In verse 20 of this passage, what four words describe the father's reunion with the son who had turned his back on him and squandered everything he had been given?

_____

_____

What does this tell you about God's love toward us, even when we fail?

_____

_____

In the father of the prodigal son, we can see a picture of God's passionate, undying love for us. Day after day, the father patiently waited for his son to come home. In the same way, our heavenly Father also patiently waits for us to turn away from the demands of the world and spend some time with Him. But what usually takes place at your house? When the Wonderful Counselor comes knocking on the door of your heart, do you let Him in or tell Him to take a number?! I must confess that I've done both!

Read Mark 12:28–31.
Have you ever found yourself so busy doing things for everyone else that your time with God disappears?

_____

Do you ever allow other people's opinions of how you should spend your time to take priority over what you feel God wants you to do?

_____

How can you avoid this situation in the future?

_____

_____

_____

Notice that this passage in Mark doesn't say, "_First_ love your neighbor, and then, if time allows, love God." _Our relationship with God must always come first._ In fact, loving God first is the _only way_ we will find the strength to unconditionally love others. It's _His_ love that must flow through _us_.

Knowing that, how important is our quiet time with God?

_____

_____

Our quiet time with God is our lifeline! It's only through spending time in His presence that we get filled with His love and can then reach out to others with the fresh overflow of that love in our hearts.

As the saying goes, living a victorious Christian life isn't about imitation; it's about inhabitation. It's not me, but "Christ _in_ me, the hope of glory" (see Colossians 1:27), that will make a difference in the lives of those around me. Of course I need to obey Him and cooperate with His work in me, but the power to do that comes only through spending time with Him in prayer and in His Word. Otherwise we become like taxi drivers who don't take time to fill up with gas because they're too busy! Before the day is out, they're out of gas and can no longer be of service to anyone else. Without daily time with God, we will spend our days running on empty.

Read Romans 12:1–2.
Notice that little word, _be_, in the first sentence in verse 2. Does this verse instruct us to change ourselves, or will something else change us?

_____

_____

What's the difference between trying to change ourselves, and being changed?

_____

_____

According to verse 2, what will this change help us discover?

_____

_____

On our own, we can't manufacture God's love and power whenever we need them. Our time spent with God must be point A on our journey with Him; it's His heavenly headquarters from which we get our marching orders and the equipment we need to carry out His plan. _Spending time with God in His Word and in prayer are the secrets to living a powerful life!_

Read Acts 4:13.

Which "self-help seminar" had the disciples attended that made them so effective? Who was their Teacher?

_____

_____

In reality, what two vital qualifications did they *lack*, from the world's perspective? What characteristic did they exhibit that made up for it, and how did they acquire that characteristic?

_____

_____

How might that encourage you in your walk with God?

_____

_____

Sometimes people are fooled into thinking that if they sign up for a popular seminar or read a particular book, it will substitute for their private time with God. But let me ask you this: Can reading a steamy romance novel substitute for spending time with your husband? Of course not!

When we let our time with God slip away, no matter how good our intentions, we're forced to try to live the life of the Spirit in the strength of the flesh. It will never work! We'll *never* produce lasting fruit in the strength of the flesh. That's why we needed a Savior in the first place! Living in our own strength is like writing a check with no money in the bank, or plugging into a socket that has not been connected to the electricity. *We must exchange God's supernatural love and power for any shred of goodness that we can muster up on our own.* "Loving our neighbors as ourselves" truly comes about *only* when we are filled with God's love first, and then *He reaches through us* to touch others.

Do you want true love? Peace? Direction? Strength to get through a tough time? Hope that things will get better? Wisdom that will guide you in making a decision? How about a free "therapy session" with the Wonderful Counselor? A personal audience with the Creator of the universe is an awesome privilege, no matter how busy your day may be! Let's guard that time, and come into His presence with joy!

2. OVERCOMMITMENT AFFECTS OUR RELATIONSHIP WITH OUR HUSBANDS.

That's right! That guy on the other side of the newspaper deserves more of our time than our girlfriends do! You are his companion, his helper (a.k.a. his "executive vice-president"), and hopefully his best friend. *Distractions that constantly claim the time that our marriages need to thrive are dangerous.* That's why so many affairs begin in the first place. There may not be a lack of love, but rather there may be a lack of the time together that is absolutely necessary to keep that relationship fresh and satisfying.

Let's take a minute to consider how the use of our time can either support or sabotage our marriage.

Read Proverbs 12:4 and 19:13.
Do your actions honor your husband, or drive him crazy the way a dripping faucet might?!

_____

What are some ways in which you could save some energy to invest in your marriage?

_____

_____

SUPERWOMAN DOESN'T EXIST!

We get some funny ideas sometimes. Most of us think that we should be Christian "superwomen." You know exactly what I mean: able to hold down a seventy-hour-a-week $90K-a-year job; raise three kids, one of whom is in soccer, one in the band, and one taking ballet lessons; teach Sunday school each week; prepare home-cooked meals every night; lead two Bible studies; and keep up a Martha Stewart *Living* home; all while you run a shelter for the homeless on the side! If you can do all that, then congratulations! You are Superwoman after all!

Unfortunately, many of us seem to place this type of standard on ourselves. It's so easy to think we need to take part in every single opportunity that comes our way. We tend to take on way too many commitments, then wonder why we are stressed to the max, why our homes have turned into battlefields and our marriages grow more distant and less exciting by the day. I wonder how many marriages end simply because of boredom, because no one took the time to keep them vibrant and exciting.

Marriage was designed by God to be a loving, growing, supportive, *fun* partnership between equals! Let's see what God had to say about the original marriage — before it was tainted by sin.

Read Genesis 1:26–28.

According to verse 27, whom did God create in His image?

_____

According to verse 28, whom did He tell to rule?

_____

Was the woman deemed any less important in God's plan for the earth? Why or why not?

_____

_____

Do you believe God thinks you're as valuable and useful in His kingdom as a man? Why or why not?

_____

_____

Notice that God didn't talk directly to Adam, and then send a copy of the memo to Eve! Both the husband and wife were important and capable in His eyes, although as we'll see later, their roles were different. This understanding of God's love and esteem for women enables us to freely pass that honor on to our husbands, without striving and competing for "our rights" in the marriage. God's idea of marriage isn't about position; it's about oneness and mutual respect.[1] We don't have to prove anything! But we are called to love, honor, and serve our husbands just as we love, honor, and serve the Lord.

So raise your hand if you're perfect. Hmm . . . no takers? Well, guess what? Neither are our husbands! All joking aside, I think we'd be amazed at the results if we'd voluntarily put our husband's needs first once in a while. *God will honor a woman who honors her husband, and in turn, most husbands will return the favor.* Regardless of whether or not it's "politically correct" these days, kindness and a servant's heart have always been God's plan.

But beware — the reverse is also true. If your hubby's needs are always last on your list, even behind more "spiritual" commitments, watch out. You're on dangerous ground, even in a Christian marriage. Our husbands deserve more than our leftovers. I challenge you to be true to your higher priorities and *choose* to save time to invest in your marriage. In the long run, the distractions in our lives are meaningless when compared to preserving a lifelong marriage.

3. Overcommitment Affects Our Family Relationships.

Let's consider the home front. Is the love of Christ demonstrated there? Is there peace? (Notice I didn't say "quiet" — a noisy home can still be a peaceful home.) Is there mutual support? A sense of unity? Is there time set aside for family fun? Is there time allotted to plant the Word of God in your children's hearts?

I don't know about you, but if there has ever been anything challenging in my life, it is raising three kids! There have been days when, if I didn't have God's help, I'd hide behind the couch and wave the white flag! I need God's help and wisdom, His patience and diligence, and that's just to get through breakfast!

Without God's help, I'd be a miserable failure as a mom. With it, however, I have the strength to keep doing all I can to raise my children to become godly adults, to come alongside them and point them to the Cross. Not that I'm even close to perfect, but this one thing I know for certain: His love makes all the difference!

Read Matthew 16:26 aloud.
Now read it aloud again, substituting the word *family* for *soul*.

What would you be willing to trade for your family? Does your Daytimer support your answer?

_____

What things are you tempted to do before meeting the needs of your family? How can you work around these distractions to better meet their needs?

_____

_____

_____

We pay a high price when everyone else's needs come before our family's needs, when leaving them in the dust becomes our unintentional choice. Please understand that I am not pointing fingers. I've been there myself! When we sense God moving in our hearts, we want to share it with the world! We're filled with ideas of how we can help this person or encourage that person, and that is wonderful. The danger comes when we do all that without saving enough time and energy for our families. I'm convinced that God will lead us to do *both*, but we have to be led by the Spirit.

I find myself torn between these two commitments on a daily basis, and I have to reel myself back to God's priorities for me. *It doesn't matter if I'm Mother Teresa away from home, my family deserves a mom who is there when they need me.* I have *one* shot in this life to enjoy them and make a difference in their lives, and I want to seize the moment! How about you?

Read Titus 2:3–5.

On the chart below, list the "dos" and "don'ts" that are outlined for older women (mature believers) in verses 3 and 4. Then list the "dos" and "don'ts" for the younger women (newer Christians) given in verses 4 and 5.

	OLDER WOMEN	YOUNGER WOMEN
DOS	_____	_____
	_____	_____
	_____	_____
DON'TS	_____	_____
	_____	_____
	_____	_____

What can happen if we *don't* do these things?

_____

From this passage, how can your actions and attitudes towards your family be an integral part of your walk with God?

_____

_____

Some versions state in this passage that we "dishonor," or even "blaspheme" God's Word by not honoring our families! Such stern warnings compel us to examine our own family situations. Are you truly honoring God by honoring each member of your family?

_____

_____

_____

These principles from Titus 2 will be reflected throughout this whole study of balance in our lives. Throughout the coming weeks, we'll learn how to practically implement this passage in our priorities and the daily choices we make. We'll discuss how to really love our husbands and children, how to be sensible with our use of time and resources, how to keep our motives pure, how to become efficient household managers, how to be kind — even when our feelings tell us to do otherwise, how to honor our husbands by allowing them to lead, and how to truly "walk the talk." If we learn these lessons, our lives won't bring shame to the cause of Christ, but will instead bring glory to His name!

It's so important that our children and husbands know they are *precious* to us, second only to God, not the hundreds of other things that can overload our schedules. It's so easy to miss out on the priceless childhood years! They are part of that "one shot" to influence our kids, to show them affection, to instruct and discipline and build character that will shape their lives forever. Like marks in wet cement, whatever we say and do sticks!

Think about this: The influence of a loving mother will stay with her children the rest of their lives, and be passed on to their children. *There are no substitutes for a loving relationship with parents, or for biblically based parenting:* not toys or possessions, not activities or sports, not freedom from boundaries or elaborate vacations. *A mother's shaping love and discipline is a treasured investment in her children's lives for years to come.*

I believe our children don't really want *things* as much as they want *us!* I'd even go so far as to say that most kids would choose time with their parents over the hundred and one other "opportunities for growth" that we feel are so important for their lives. They just want to know they are loved, period. And that's what we moms do best, that is, when we're not killing ourselves by cramming a thousand other things into our schedules!

At times good parenting requires us to say "no" to someone else's demands, and "yes" to the needs of our children. At other times we need to say "no" to the children so we can meet the needs of someone else! *Both* are essential parts of the big picture if we want to raise children who know they are loved dearly by God and by us, and yet raise them to become God-centered instead of self-centered. *The secret is in knowing "when to say when."* Easier said than done! (We'll address this issue again in a later chapter.)

4. Overcommitment Affects Our Relationship with Others.

Let me just tell it like it is. When we're living life close to God and spending time with Him, we just do things better. We love better, we serve more effectively, and our lives are more focused and fruitful. *When we get distracted and ignore our private time with God, the very people we are striving to serve get second best.*

We blow it when we don't spend time with Jesus first every day. We have no words of life to share. We offer them yesterday's manna, instead of the God-directed words and deeds meant to meet their specific needs. Remember the taxi driver? *We try to fill their tanks when we're both running on empty.*

Yet this is a tricky balance because God's heart is that we lay down our lives for others. Life's problems are all around us every day, ready or not. But when we're not in the habit of spending time with God, all we have to offer them are our own fickle opinions rather than the flawless wisdom of God's Word. One can change a life; the other can't. Which would you rather hear from a friend when you're struggling?

Read 2 Timothy 3:16–17.
According to these verses, in what five ways can the Bible help us through life's challenges?

_____

_____

Why would sharing God's Word with someone be more helpful than just sharing your own opinions?

_____

_____

_____

As women, God seems to work in our lives in seasons. Whether we're single, married, have pre-school or school-aged children, or are empty-nesters, life hands us a new deck to deal during each of these times. God gives us an avenue of service for a while, and we learn and grow in it as we work. Then He opens another window of opportunity to teach us something new, and so it goes.

Yet we forget that although the Bible teaches that there's a time for everything (see Ecclesiastes 3), *not everything has to be done at the same time!* That's good news! God promises to give us the strength we need to do the things *He* directs us to do each day. Do you think the Proverbs 31 woman did all of that in one week? If she did, there was another resurrection story that someone forgot to write about!

When God changes the direction in our lives, it often requires us to let some things go to make room for our new responsibilities. We can choose to either give up a thing or two, or we can keep heaping commitments on our plates until we're mad at the world and eventually lose our sanity! Sometimes we mistakenly keep taking on more, convinced we must be doing the godly thing. *But in reality, we may be acting more like Pharisees than disciples, choosing to look good on the outside, while dying on the inside.* Ironically that's when those around us lose out, because of our lack of obedience. (Ouch!)

Read Matthew 23:27–28.
Since it's not necessarily wrong "to look beautiful on the outside," where did the Pharisees cross the line into disobedience?

_____

_____

How do you sometimes slip into this same sin? How can you guard against it?

_____

_____

There are also times that by saying yes to everything, we actually rob someone else of an opportunity to grow, whether it is through working in the nursery or in teaching a Bible study. However unintentional, *we hinder* others from trying their wings, often while grumbling about how we always get stuck doing everything! What's wrong with that picture?! Of course, there's a time to hang in there and be faithful when we don't feel like it, but there's also a time to let go and move on. It all comes back to listening for God's direction. Only He knows how much we can handle, and when we need to say "when!"

BACK TO THE BASICS

When we forget God's priorities for us of loving Him and loving our families, we become restless, depressed, and overwhelmed. The joy of serving others fades, and the delightful determination to give it our all is replaced by the day-to-day drudgery of just getting it done. We experience a constant inner turmoil, and a gentle tugging by the Holy Spirit to get our lives in order. Left unchecked, overcommitment can cause us to lose the respect of our spouses and families, not to mention intimacy with our heavenly Father.

Read Ephesians 5:15–17.
Again, what three things are we instructed to do in these verses, and how can we practically implement them?

_____

_____

No matter how busy we are, we need to *make* time to hear from God and be strengthened by Him, and *make* time to actively love our families. Just love God and love people! Jesus said that when we fulfill these two commandments, we fulfill the whole Law. Sure, it takes continual juggling, and many things have to be forfeited or wait for another day or season, *but getting everything done isn't the right goal. Staying on God's course is!* We can trust God to meet our needs and the needs of others most effectively if we just let go and let God be in charge of our commitments.

Bottom line? If we live by God's priorities, we will accomplish the most important things in life. And that's all that really matters!

PRAYER

Father, You know my schedule and how out of balance things can get at times. You also know my good intentions and how I sincerely want to live according to Your plan. Help me to get filled up with Your love first each day, and then love my family and friends through the overflow of Your love within me. Help me seize each moment for Your glory. In Jesus' name. Amen.

SUMMARY POINTS

• Our relationships with God, our husbands, our children, and others are negatively affected when we're stretched too thin.
• There are no substitutes for a mother's shaping influence on her family.
• Rather than to get everything done, our goal must be to stay on God's specific course for our lives.

FROM PRINT TO POWER: PERSONAL APPLICATION

1. In your journal, reflect on the strength of the following relationships in your life:

A. GOD: Do you spend time with Him every day? Do you ever allow the needs of others to steal your time with Him? Do you truly know His love for you? Do you try to obey His Word?

B. HUSBAND: Do you feel good about your marriage? Is a busy schedule ever divisive between you and your spouse? Do you ever set aside time to do special things for him, or does your relationship usually get overlooked between the kids and other commitments?

C. FAMILY: Does your lifestyle reflect your attitude toward your children as that of treasures or tag-alongs? Is the atmosphere of your home warm and loving, or hectic and irritable? Do your words and actions truly convey how much you love them?

D. OTHERS: Do you feel like you have a handle on balancing your friendships with your other commitments? Do you sometimes feel you're taken advantage of just because you're a willing worker? Are you able to say "no" when you need to?

2. Throughout this week, ask God to make you aware of things that may need to be added to or eliminated from your schedule. Write these things down, and begin to take action to work them out of your routine. Then ask Him to lead you into all He has planned for you during this season of your life. It's exciting to live by faith!

THE PLAN

SECTION TWO

CHAPTER 4

CHARTING YOUR COURSE

"Run in such a way as to get the prize."

— 1 Corinthians 9:24

As we begin the "planning" section of this study, let's review what we've discussed so far. We started with the story of Mary and Martha, and found that although Martha wanted to *do things* for Jesus, He really just wanted a *relationship* with her. We also conceded that the only way we'll ever change is to abide in God's strength and allow Him to do His work through us.

Next, we examined our lives by comparing them to God's model woman described in Proverbs 31. By adapting that passage to fit today's lifestyle, we were able to zero in on some practical areas in which we could use some work! We discussed the difference between being led by the Spirit in serving others and allowing our time to be eaten up by meaningless commitments. Through that, we learned the importance of guarding the time and energy we need to accomplish the things we're called to do. We also acknowledged the stress and frustration that build in our homes when we constantly say "yes" to everyone without praying about our commitments first, squeezing out the time we desperately need with God and our families.

In this chapter we'll build on these discoveries as we begin to establish new priorities and goals. We'll discover how using God's Word and some strategic planning can keep us on track. We'll examine how we spend our time, and how we can better line up our lives to accomplish God's will. Lastly, we'll determine how we can integrate our goals into our daily schedules, making us more focused and organized women of God!

So never fear! There's hope for even the craziest of schedules. I should know — I'm living proof!

In a sentence or two, share a thought that has challenged you so far in this study, as well as how it has affected your daily life.

_____

_____

_____

As we attempt to carry out God's will, we need more than basic time management skills. Let's face it: *We need help!* And I know just the source for that help. Think of it this way: If my van breaks down, I raise the hood, get out the owner's manual, and pretend I have some clue as to what I'm looking for. . . . Okay, so maybe that's not such a great example!

The point is that God holds the patent on the human race, and His Word is our owner's manual! The Bible has all the answers we need — we just need to learn how to find them. Most people would pay any price to have the answers to life, and we have them all contained in one volume! God's Word is a both a gift and a necessity to us.

RUNNING THE RACE TO WIN

Earlier in this study, we read a passage of scripture in which the apostle Paul compared living for Christ to running a race. In some versions he refers to it as having *"finished my course"* (2 Timothy 4:7 KJV). To me, this wording speaks of following a specific route, a plan of action, or an agenda that God has laid out for each of us. I believe that we come to the "starting line" when we begin to seek God for what He wants us to do. Once we understand what the course will be, we can then begin running, trusting God to lead us all the way to the finish line and accomplish His work in us.

Read 2 Timothy 4:7–8 and 1 Corinthians 9:24–25.
Summarize what each of these verses says to you about your "race." What "race" are you currently running, or feeling drawn toward? Explain.

_____

_____

_____

_____

_____

Doing absolutely everything cannot be our goal. Running God's race for us must be the goal. Working toward our heavenly crown of righteousness should be a greater motivation to us than just "getting everything done" here on earth. That fact encourages me, because we simply can't do it all! At times I look around and see women who seem to be able to do everything and do it well — they have the perfect house, the perfect children, the perfect size and shape, the perfect career, even the perfect relationship with God, and I just want to give up! But guess what — you can't see every area of their lives, and you don't know what goes on in the secret places of their hearts.

Despite what other people around you may be doing, I have good news! *You're not called to be perfect in every single area. You're called to run the race that God has set before you!* You're accountable only for what God's called you to do. You can't live their lives and yours too! Sure, God wants our lives to shine with excellence as a testimony of His power to change us, and we should all strive to do that for His glory. But that's *excellence,* not *perfection.* There's a huge difference!

I learned this lesson the hard way once while I was preparing to host a huge party. As I worked to the point of exhaustion, I heard that still, small voice whisper, *A clean house is a good testimony, but a perfect house is a waste of time.* I believe that is true across the board. We should all strive for excellence in everything that we do so that we can show forth the character of God, *but obsessing over everything while trying to reach perfection is a tool of the enemy!* Because we will never reach perfection in this lifetime, that lifestyle will keep us perpetually frustrated! It also keeps our minds focused on the things of this world instead of the things of God. We simply can't afford to follow that path.

The same is true with regard to trying to fulfill someone else's calling. Chasing the elusive dream of being just like someone else is a disappointing dead end. It just won't happen! That's because *God has gifted you to be you, and you probably have your hands full doing that right, without trying to be Miss America on the side!*

I say all this because it's vital that we don't become too "hung up" on stuff we're *not* called to do! There's an old saying that goes something like this: "Where *God* guides, He provides." In other words, when we're on God's errand, He will supply what we need. So as we map out our priorities and goals, let's keep in mind that we don't have to be everything to everyone. In other words, *all you have to do is do what God has called you to do.*

Period! If you're not Martha Stewart, that's okay — you're simply called to follow Christ. Now *that's* good news!

Read 2 Timothy 2:20–21.

According to verse 21, what three things describe a "vessel of honor" (NASB)?

_____

_____

_____

What do these things mean to you?

_____

_____

_____

How does verse 21 tell us we can become one?

_____

_____

_____

How does this passage fit in with our learning to become more focused and fruitful?

_____

_____

_____

_____

ESTABLISHING BALANCED LIVES

The greatest counsel in the world won't do us any good if it is never applied. So let's begin the process of integrating these truths into our lives by mapping out a three-part plan to stay on track with God. To do this, we'll need to:

1. Set our priorities.

2. Set realistic, measurable goals.

3. Create a plan as to how to incorporate those goals into our daily routines.

When we're done, we'll be able to see where we are, where we're headed, and the steps we need to take to get there.

STEP #1: ESTABLISH PRIORITIES.

Take a minute to jot down the things that are *most* important in your life in the space below. It might help to ask yourself these questions: To whom, and to what, has God called **you** to be faithful? When you meet Him face to face, what things will He ask you about? Who are the most important people in your life, and how have you been called to influence them? Are there specific things you feel called to do? What are they? *Once you've established "who" and "what" should be your most important priorities, you can then set goals to achieve those ends first, and then line up the rest of life around those treasures.*

I know this can seem intimidating. You may be thinking, *I have no idea what God wants to do in my life!* That's okay! Most of the time, God reveals His plans to us little by little as we take steps of obedience to follow Him. Just write what you feel in your heart.

What are your priorities?

_____

_____

STEP #2: SET ATTAINABLE GOALS.

Think of it this way: My *priorities* are what I *think* and *feel* are the most important to me. My *goals,* then, are what I will *do* to live by those priorities. Goals are the plans and actions I will take that keep my life centered on my priorities. Without goals, we would have no targets. We would never have the joy of saying, "By the grace of God, I did it!" We limit our fruitfulness when we're disorganized and distracted. In a nutshell, God wants to use each of us in His divine plan — a plan that's too good to miss — and after some prayer, setting goals is a great place to start!

Read Philippians 3:10–14.
What was the apostle Paul's goal in life? (See verse 10.) What three things did he admonish us to do to meet our goals? (See verses 13–14.)

_____

_____

_____

Knowing Paul's past, which included persecuting Christians, how does verse 13 encourage you to "forget what lies behind"? Explain how you could apply, or have applied, Paul's strategy in your life.

_____

_____

_____

_____

A good goal needs to be:

1. **Measurable:** Can you tell when you've reached it?

2. **Realistic:** With God's help and your effort, is it within reach at this time in your life? Will it stretch your faith? Is it realistic in your circumstances?

3. **Practical:** When you achieve it, will you be a better person? Does it line up with God's Word and your priorities?[1]

Although most of us live life in the fast lane, *when it comes to reaching goals, a lack of time isn't always our real source of frustration. More often it's a lack of focus.* We confuse activity with accomplishment, and busyness with productivity. Yet with clear direction and some time restraints, we're more prone to stay focused and get more done. Best of all, we have more time to enjoy life because our time will be better spent. As Pastor John Palmer says, "Just pretend you're leaving for Hawaii in the morning, and you will be amazed how much you can accomplish today!"[2]

Read John 17:4 and 9:4.

According to John 17:4, what was Jesus' ultimate goal while He was on the earth?

_____

_____

How can the principle given in John 9:4 be applied to your life?

_____

_____

Spiritual goals cover such things as Bible reading, prayer, scripture memorization, personal evangelism, encouragement, and ministry. For example, you might ask yourself, *What would I like to set for my personal Bible study goal this year?* You could read for ten minutes a day, read a chapter or two each day, go through the whole Bible in a year, or concentrate more on in-depth chapter studies. You can set similar goals with prayer, fellowship, hospitality, or any other spiritual matter. The point is to begin a habit that you can *continue,* and set some realistic goals.

What spiritual goals have you set for yourself? Is there a time of day or another system that works best for you to read your Bible, for example? If you have children, how do you work around their schedules?

_____

_____

_____

_____

What other goals could you set for your life at this time?

_____

_____

_____

STEP #3: INTEGRATE THESE GOALS INTO YOUR DAILY LIFE.

I tend to be one of those people who think that I can squeeze way too much into a day and still come out smelling like a rose. In reality, if I'm not being led by the Spirit to do all those things, by the end of the day I am more like a loaded cannon that is ready to blow!

The paradox is this: When we're walking in God's strength and doing what He calls us to do, we can accomplish tremendous amounts of work — far above what we could do in our natural abilities. Yet when our spiritual ears are dull and we agree to too many unnecessary commitments, someone will eventually bear the brunt of our exhaustion. When our schedules are crammed, often our quiet time — the very place we receive the strength and direction we need — is the first to go.

I've learned the hard way that the only way to be effective as a Christian is to live according to *God's* agenda (not mine), in *God's* ability (not mine), and for *God's* glory (not my own). Remember, this life is not about us! It's about *Him!* Life is about how I fit into *God's* eternal purposes, not how He can bless *my* efforts to be a successful Christian!

Think about that last statement for a moment. What's the difference between your fitting in with God's purposes and asking Him to bless your own efforts? How might this challenge your thinking?

_____

_____

_____

_____

The first outlook focuses on me; the second focuses on God. *God is the One who can fit all the pieces of all the puzzles of all the lives of all His children together into one gigantic tapestry, and it comes out beautifully in the end!*

List several ways in which you can begin to reach the goals that you have set for yourself. How will you continue to ensure that these goals line up with what *God* wants you to do? Be sure to be practical and realistic.

_____

_____

_____

_____

WHERE DOES THE TIME GO?

A week is made up of exactly 168 hours. Where does the time go? Let's follow a few simple steps to answer that question!

Take a few minutes to list the commitments that make up your non-discretionary time — all of the time that is already spoken for. This would include how many hours you need to sleep, work, follow through with church commitments, maintain your quiet time, do the grocery shopping, prepare meals, do the laundry, transport the kids, help the kids with homework, etc. This will give you a realistic view of what's involved in your routine that, for all intents and purposes, is fixed.

Next, add up those hours, and subtract them from 168. How many of your hours are spoken for? What is left over is what we'll call your "discretionary" time, that is, the hours in which you have some flexibility. Once you have calculated this answer, you can set your priorities to better use what time you do have available.

We choose how we manage our discretionary time. Do you feel like you're being a good steward of the time you've been given?

_____

_____

Is there some new activity in which you want to invest some time that you're not currently doing now? Explain.

_____

_____

_____

_____

By looking at the results of your calculations, would you say you're basically living within your priorities? Are you scheduling some time for the things that are important to you, as well as time to work toward your goals? When you compare your weekly commitments with your priorities and goals, are they in sync with your understanding of God's will for you during this season of your life? Or do they just fill up your hours? Finally, are you on course to accomplish whatever it is that burns inside of you, or are you allowing whatever is most urgent to dictate your schedule? _I'm not talking about ignoring your children to pursue goals. I'm talking about making conscious decisions as to how you use your time every day._

Write your thoughts regarding these questions below.

_____

_____

_____

_____

_____

As a side note, I know that when your home is full of little ones, or teenagers for that matter, keeping realistic schedules seems impossible! I remember days when I barely had time to take a shower, let alone accomplish any goals! When you have young children, some of your realistic goals may simply be taking time to read to them or nurture them in some way each day. Those are worthy pursuits! _If that's what God is calling you to do now,_ *then do it with all your heart, and don't feel guilty about not "accomplishing more"!* Life comes to us in seasons, and babies don't keep!

Read Ecclesiastes 3:1–8.

What does verse 1 promise us?

_____

_____

_____

Are there things that you feel God may want you to add to your schedule now, or at a later time? Explain.

_____

_____

_____

_____

There is a time for everything, and a season for every activity under heaven. I know that may seem hard to believe, but God's Word doesn't lie! And with a bit of advance planning, there should be an hour or two each week in which you could squeeze something just for you, possibly by trading children with a friend, or getting up extra early. If you're willing to make the effort, an hour here or there to just unwind and relax will do you a world of good.

A good reality check for me is to compare my lifetime goals and priorities with today's calendar. Have I spent time with God today? Are my obligations things that line up with what is really important to me, or have I said yes to something simply because that was easier than saying no? Granted, some of the invitations we accept are simply to reach out to others, and those are important. Others are just for fun, and that's okay too. *It's when we take on commitments that cause us to frequently neglect our own needs, our families, or our time with God, that things get out of balance.*

If you add up 364 more days just like the one you're in the middle of today, you will have a pretty good indication of what's really important in your life!

Read Ephesians 2:8–10.

As we begin to set our priorities and goals, and determine how to make them happen in our lives, what two things in verses 8 and 9 can we not afford to forget?

_____

_____

According to verse 10, why should we use our time so carefully?

_____

_____

Our good works will never buy us a ticket to heaven. Yet we were *created* to do them! Do you realize that *you* were created to accomplish specific things in God's kingdom? You're hardly a nobody when the King of kings has *designed you from scratch* to accomplish things just for Him.

Remember, the other *huge* element in this equation is that when we have an intimate relationship with God, His supernatural power can flow through us to accomplish things far greater than we ever could without Him. When we come to the end of our natural abilities and begin to lean hard on God, we set the stage for Him to do things through us that are far beyond our skills and talents. Remember Moses at the edge of the Red Sea? If he had never been in a position of such great need, he never would have seen God move in such an awesome way! *All this planning is meant to do is to help us clear away the clutter in our schedules, so we can use our time for His glory!*

PRINCIPLES TO HELP US STAY ON COURSE

The following is a list of seven principles designed to help us accomplish God's specific plan for us. As you review them, take a mental inventory of how you're doing.

1. DON'T BE FOOLED BY YOUR GOOD INTENTIONS.

The best intentions, no matter how genuine they may be, are not the same as accomplishments. In other words, "It ain't over 'til it's over!" Those magical "somedays," when circumstances are in perfect order and free time is plentiful, rarely come. If we wait for them, we'll never tackle jobs God intends for us to do today.

Read Matthew 25:1–13.

How many of the virgins wanted to go with the Bridegroom?

_____

What prevented some from going?

_____

What can you learn from this story about being prepared and then acting on what you know to do?

_____

_____

2. PLAN AHEAD.

Read Luke 14:28–30.

Are you a "planner" or a "free spirit"?

_____

How might planning work together with being led by the Spirit?

_____

_____

I don't know about you, but I picture this man in Jesus' parable sitting at his desk with a cup of coffee. Scratching his head while pouring over a Daytimer and a calculator, he's trying to come up with a plan to get the tower up on schedule and within his budget. Sound familiar? *Coming up with a workable plan can be the most important part of a building project.* Where would a builder be without a blueprint? It's really the only way to get from Point A to Point B with any kind of efficiency. The same is true as we endeavor to do things for God. Careful planning makes all the difference.

3. YIELD TO GOD'S TIMING.

In order to live your life in God's strength, He has to be in the lead. Your self-determination alone won't cut it. It's got to be *His* work in you, done *His* way, in *His* timing. Always remember, God's timing, like the rest of His nature, is perfect!

I've heard it said that life is like a parade. We see only what's directly ahead of us and behind us, but God sees the whole thing as if from the Goodyear blimp! That's why His timing is so trustworthy. *He sees the big picture, and He alone knows exactly what we need and when we need it!* The key is to submit all that we do to Him, and let Him make sense of it all.

Read Acts 8:26–38.

Think about the importance of the timing of Philip's divine appointment. What might have happened if Philip had debated with God, or decided to put it off for a few days?

_____

_____

Share about a time when obeying God's timing was crucial for you. What were the results of your obedience?

_____

_____

_____

This Ethiopian eunuch has been said to have brought the gospel to the whole continent of Africa! But his opportunity to hear the gospel hinged on Philip's *immediate obedience,* even though Philip didn't know exactly what God was up to. *Only when we act in God's timing will there truly be "a time for everything."* A time to work hard and a time to ride bikes with the kids, a time for Bible study and a time to clean closets! God is very practical. We will experience the fullness of His promises only in the fullness of His timing. So relax — God knows what He's doing!

4. FINISH WHAT YOU START.

Read Acts 20:24.

How might God be glorified when we finish what we start?

_____

If there's something you've been putting off that you feel is important to finish, what changes could you make in your schedule that would make that possible?

_____

_____

When this life is over, there will still be more things on our desks to do, more laundry, more unfinished projects, and missed opportunities. But by the grace of God, we will be able to say with Paul, "I have finished the race." As we're faithful in the small things, God will enable us to finish the race that He's mapped out for us. We continue to press on, hoping one day to hear the words: *"Well done, good and faithful servant! You have been faithful with a few things; I will put you in charge of many things. Come and share your master's happiness!"* (Matthew 25:21). That's what it's all about!

5. KNOW WHEN TO SAY "WHEN."

Read Mark 1:32–38.

Have you ever felt pressured to be two places at once? Jesus did! According to verse 33, how many people wanted His attention?

_____

What led Him to go against popular opinion and change His direction?

_____

What can we learn from His example?

_____

_____

_____

I often find myself at a crossroads. Is what I'm working on worth the effort it will take to do it well? Shall I do what it takes to finish it with excellence, or would my time be better spent on something else?

How do we make those tough decisions? The same way Jesus did: We need to hear from God.

6. SUBMIT YOUR PLANS TO GOD.

Read Luke 22:41–42.

What can we learn from Jesus' prayer in this passage?

_____

_____

_____

_____

When that prayer is hard for you to pray, what might you remind yourself about God's character that will make it easier?

_____

_____

Those seven little words — *"Not my will, but yours be done"* — should be the basis of our entire prayer life. God is in control, and He always has our best interests at heart. *His will for us is always for our best. We can bank on it!* In times of doubt, we would do well to remember that He loves us so much, and He understands us more than we could ever understand ourselves.

7. BE ACCOUNTABLE.

Read Ephesians 4:14–15.

According to verse 15, what will cause us to grow up?

_____

How could making ourselves accountable to other believers cause us to grow?

_____

_____

My husband Dave has this little phrase that always makes me cringe when I hear it. He says, "You're not going to want to hear this, but…" Then, *because he loves me enough to help me grow,* he points out something I'm doing, or not doing, that is not good for me. At that point, I have a choice: I can listen to him, pray about it, and make any necessary changes, or I can ignore him or get angry, and let those words of "truth" fall by the wayside. After praying, I can almost always see the truth in what he's said, the need for change, and the benefits of our honest relationship. When we make ourselves accountable to someone, God can use that person to smooth away our rough edges and ultimately cause us to become more like Him.

HELP WITH DECISIONS

The best way to make tough decisions about what deserves our time and our attention most is to weigh each option in light of eternity. You can do this by asking yourself the following three questions:

1. Do I sense God's leading in this?

2. Will it make an eternal difference in someone's life?

3. Is it consistent with God's Word and the priorities and goals I feel He has for me?[3]

If you can answer "yes" to these questions, then do it with all your heart! If your answer is "no" to more than one, then don't do it! It will just waste your time. Obviously these questions don't address the little everyday decisions in our lives, but when it comes to the more important ones, it can be very helpful to gauge your priorities as you try to decide what is best.

God knows our commitments, as well as the limits of our time and energy. He also knows where He wants to stretch us beyond our abilities. If we allow Him to, He will direct us to what's best for us, and steer us clear of worthless distractions. He is truly the "Wonderful Counselor" and the "Prince of Peace." As we set our hearts to listen for His direction, set our priorities and goals, and then diligently apply them to our daily lives, we will experience the peace — and the relief — of living balanced lives. It works!

PRAYER

Father, help me to listen for that still, small Voice within me as I make decisions regarding what I should take on or let go in my schedule. Show me Your plans and priorities for my life. Direct me this week as I establish my goals, and may Your Holy Spirit guide me so that in everything I do, I may bring glory to Your name. In Jesus' name I pray. Amen.

SUMMARY POINTS

• Since we can't do everything, our goal should be to discover God's will for our lives, and focus on fulfilling it.

• Establishing priorities and goals will help us use our time most effectively.

• Abiding by the seven principles listed can help us stay focused and help us make godly decisions.

FROM PRINT TO POWER: PERSONAL APPLICATION

Give your priorities some thought and prayer. Then, in the next several journaling pages, record your answers to the following questions:

1. *What* and *who* are most important to me, and in what order?

_____

_____

2. What do I think are some of God's purposes for my life?

_____

_____

3. The following outline was written by Pastor John Palmer. Use it to generate some ideas, personalize them according to your needs, and record them in your prayer journal. With so many different options to consider, you may want to use the entire outline or just the portions that speak to you.[4]

I. SPIRITUAL GOALS

    A. Bible reading _____

    B. Prayer _____

    C. Scripture memorization _____

    D. Personal evangelism _____

    E. Encouragement (sending notes, making phone calls, etc.) _____

    F. Ministry _____

II. FAMILY GOALS

    A. Family worship (for example, having devotions together) _____

    B. Spouse (doing something special with or for them)_____

    C. Children (spiritual, educational, recreational goals with or for them)_____

    D. Parents (keeping in touch, doing special things with or for them)_____

    E. Siblings (keeping in touch, doing special things with or for them)_____

III. PHYSICAL GOALS

    A. Exercise _____

    B. Rest_____

    C. Weight_____

IV. MENTAL GOALS

    A. Books (reading how many? on which topics?) _____

    B. Other learning aids (listening to tapes, attending classes or seminars)_____

V. PROFESSIONAL GOALS

List what you hope to accomplish this year, as well as five years from now, and ten years from now. Also list how you will get there. If you are a homemaker, set your domestic goals here.

    A._____

    B._____

    C._____

Five Years:

    A._____

    B._____

    C._____

Ten Years:

    A._____

    B._____

    C._____

VI. COMMUNITY/NEIGHBORHOOD GOALS

List how you would like to be a blessing in your neighborhood and community.

    A. Meet your neighbors_____

    B. Host a neighborhood gathering_____

    C. Invite neighbors to church_____

    D. Volunteer in school or community_____

VII. FINANCIAL GOALS

If you are married, be sure to set these in conjunction with your spouse.

    A. Income_____

    B. Budget_____

    C. Giving:

        1. Tithing_____

        2. Missions_____

        3. Other (certain ministries)_____

    D. Debt reduction _____

    E. Major purchases/Christmas budget_____

VIII. OTHER

    A._____

    B._____

    C._____

4. Now compare your weekly schedule to your priorities and goals.

• Are there changes you need to make?

• Do the things you participate in regularly line up with your goals and priorities?

• Are there commitments you need to decline, or new ones you need to take on?

• Would some minor adjustments help your daily routine?

5. Read Proverbs 12:11. The diligent man in this verse is making his dream a reality. He has a definite a goal, and he reaps an abundant harvest. Is there some direction from God you have received but have been "sitting on," without establishing goals to see it fulfilled? How much progress have you made? What changes could you make in your schedule that could bring it closer to reality? Pray about the situation and then record your answers.

_____

_____

_____

_____

_____

_____

_____

CHAPTER 5

BACK TO SQUARE ONE: MAKING A COMMITMENT TO PRAYER

"If men knew how much prayer affected things, they'd sorely regret missing the opportunity."

— Oswald Chambers

"Okay, so my life's going a hundred different directions. I'm way behind on the bills, Johnny needs new shoes for his school program tonight, I missed my deadline at work again today, the dog has fleas, my mother-in-law is coming for a visit this weekend, the house is a disaster, I have mountains of laundry, and the only food in the fridge looks like a science experiment! And let me get this straight . . . you want me to pray in the middle of all this? What, are you crazy? If only you could take a walk in my shoes . . ."

Believe me, I have. More days than I care to remember, I've been there, trying desperately to see the light of day over the countless demands on my time and energy. But those were the times in which I learned that prayer is essential — and it becomes even more essential the busier life gets. Prayer can give you the strength to get through the hard days, and give you hope that things will get better. Prayer can carry you when you have nothing left to give. It can guide you like a beacon through your darkest night. It can pick you up, dust you off, and truly put a song in your heart. *Bottom line? Prayer can be the deciding factor in your situation. It can change your life!*

Has there ever been a time when you experienced this kind of life-changing prayer, or received hope or direction from your quiet time with God? Share your experience.

_____

_____

_____

BUILDING RELATIONSHIP THROUGH PRAYER

There will never really be a "new" way to build a vibrant relationship with God. No drive-through lanes exist where we can get a large order of spiritual maturity and a side of biblical guidance to go! The truth is, even with the wealth of Christian resources that is all around us, *there will never be a substitute for spending time with God in prayer and in His Word.* How often we forget the incredible privilege we have been given to know the eternal, all-knowing, all-powerful God! So get your fingers and your Bibles ready! In this chapter and in the next, we'll be looking up a great number of scriptures and we'll learn how our quiet times with God lay an essential foundation as we build an intimate relationship with Him.

The truth is, God is looking for people just like you and me who, while we are far from perfect, will choose to live for Him. Think about that! The Creator of the universe invites us to co-labor with Him to bring about far greater things than we could ever imagine: *Thy kingdom come, Thy will be done on earth as it is in heaven.* That's what prayer is all about, and we can have front-row season tickets to the action if we want them!

Are you ready to go deeper with God, and allow Him to stretch you way out of your comfort zone? You'll never regret it! It's like hopping in the last seat on a roller coaster called Extreme Faith, with your hands up. It can be scary at times, but it is definitely the adventure of a lifetime!

So, who's up for a ride?

Read 2 Chronicles 16:9a.

What does God promise the person who gives Him her all? How does this differ from the world's understanding of God?

_____

_____

Is there an area of your life that could use some of that strength?

_____

_____

The relationship I have developed with God through prayer means more to me than I can put into words. I trust in Him as the One who gives me the very air I breathe and can take it from me any time He chooses. I stand in awe of Him as the Maker of this planet we call Earth, and the galaxies that are beyond our ability to number. I obey Him as the King of kings and Lord of lords. I thank Him endlessly for the sacrifice He made to pay the price for my sin, pursuing me even when I fought against Him.

To this same magnificent God I tell my deepest secrets and dreams, and receive tender comfort and encouragement that outweighs that of any other friend. He's my Helper, my Wonderful Counselor, my Teacher, my unshakable Rock in this crazy world, my heavenly Cheerleader, my Healer, my soon coming King, and my "Personal Trainer" in godliness! He's my everything, and _prayer is the crux of that whole relationship._ Don't ever minimize your prayer life — it's too good to miss!

Making Time to Pray

Read Luke 6:12.
From Jesus' example, what can we learn about the importance of prayer?

_____

_____

How does His example challenge you?

_____

_____

You might say that Jesus wrote the book on prayer — He did! But _even on His busiest days on earth, everything Jesus did was based on His ongoing fellowship with His heavenly Father._ There were times when everyone in the city wanted Him to do something, and He knew He needed to do something else — because of His prayer time. He consistently chose to leave the crowds and spend time seeking His Father's heart, even after giving of Himself all day long. _He made time to be with God,_ even if it meant going without sleep.

Honestly, I don't think we have a clue how much God loves us. Even more than a groom desires to spend time with his bride, God passionately wants to be with us — with you! Do you realize that? He's wild about you! He wants you to learn to lean on Him, to be changed by Him, to enjoy Him, and to worship Him. Prayer is hardly a duty! It should never become drudgery for us. It's a *privilege* we can guard and celebrate — an open invitation to spend time with the King of kings, day or night!

Read Hebrews 10:7.
What was Jesus' top priority as He planned His days?

_____

Does your own Daytimer reflect this same priority? If not, what changes might you need to make?

_____
_____
_____

Hear me on this. *It's easy to ask God to bless our own agenda, but how much better would it be to seek His plan that's already blessed?* Let's face it. Yielding control of our lives to someone else usually goes against everything within us. And yet, as we turn that habit around and *daily* let Him call the shots, we'll be amazed at the difference it will make. Why? Because God can see the whole parade! When we truly make God's will our priority, our lives will change, and He'll use us in ways that are far beyond all we could ever ask or imagine.

Read Matthew 6:25–33.
I often remind myself to "Seek first His kingdom today. . . ." Are there any practical methods you use that help you have a daily time with God? (For example, praying while you exercise, or getting up before the rest of the family.) Explain how these methods are helpful to you.

_____
_____
_____
_____
_____
_____

LEARNING TO WAIT ON GOD

Making prayer a priority isn't easy. It's a commitment that requires us to slow down and overlook the distractions that surround us. A friend of mine says that as soon as he sits down to pray, "the parade starts;" that is, a mental parade of all the things he needs to do starts to march through his head. Sound familiar? He has since learned to keep a notepad handy so that when the "parade" starts, he can jot those things down, put them out of his mind, and get on with his prayer time.

Sadly, for many of us, rather than waiting for the almighty God to speak to us, our prayer time has been reduced to the recitation of a list of concerns and complaints. I remember during a time of frustration when I asked God why I could never seem to hear His direction. Instantly I heard His familiar voice: "Because every time I open My mouth, you're out the door!" Ouch! But it was true. I was in and out of my prayer times faster than a NASCAR driver makes a pit stop. There was no learning taking place, no refining, no refreshment from being in God's presence. I was simply "doing my Christian duty," or so I thought, while I was practically ignoring a priceless relationship with my Maker. What a waste.

Waiting on God means just that: waiting! We must wait for Him to teach us about things that we don't understand and give us encouragement or direction through the Scriptures. Even though spending time waiting on God runs contrary to our culture, its rewards are priceless.

Read Luke 11:5–13.

If we persist in prayer, what promises are given to us?

_____

_____

What principle can we learn from the example given in this passage?

_____

_____

_____

Is there anything in your life that you feel God may want to accomplish, but will only take place through this type of persistent prayer? What would that be? What is hindering it from taking place?

_____

_____

_____

Isn't it wonderful when our prayers get answered quickly? Wouldn't it be nice if they all did? It would sure *feel* great, but it wouldn't be very beneficial for building our character. Waiting on God strengthens our relationship with Him, as we learn to trust Him on a daily basis.

God will usually answer our prayers in three ways: "yes," "no," and "wait." All three of these answers are given for *His* glory and *our* benefit. When our prayers are according to His will, He answers yes! Sometimes there are situations when what we are praying for is His will, but the timing is not yet right. Always remember that God's timing is perfect, just like the rest of His character, and some prayers may take years to be answered before we see a change. When that's the case, we must continue seeking the mind of Christ, and make sure that what we're asking for is truly God's will, and not just our own.

But when our requests don't line up with God's will, His answer will be "no." Whatever His answer, we can still be sure that God knows what He's doing and has our best interests at heart. When I really think about it, I'm so glad that God hasn't said yes to *all* of my prayers — aren't you? We can always rest in the fact that our Father sees the big picture, and He truly knows best!

WHY GOD ALLOWS TRIALS

Scripture teaches that there are times when God allows us to go through trials in order to accomplish His higher purposes in our lives. Romans 8:28 tells us, *in all things God works for the good of those who love him, who have been called according to his purpose.* He will somehow use the circumstances in our lives for good, even when that seems impossible, because His ways are higher than our ways.

Four years ago, our family felt God leading us to step out in faith to move to Florida from Iowa. This decision meant that Dave would have to leave a lucrative seventeen-year career in management at the company where he worked, for a less promising job. Yet we were sure of God's leading, even though we didn't know a soul in Florida.

We made the move, and all seemed well as Dave quickly began climbing the corporate ladder within the new company. But a year and a half later, when the company was severely downsized, his new position was suddenly eliminated. As I tried to make sense of why this had happened, God began to challenge me again with that scripture (Romans 8:28). Did I really believe it? And if I did, *was I willing to base my life on it, and trust that God knew what He was doing?*

Little did we know that God was using what looked so discouraging to open the door for Dave to go into the full-time ministry — a dream we'd shared since we first met. God truly worked all things together for our good and for His glory, even through some very trying circumstances, and we can now look back on those months as a faith-building landmark in our lives.

An amazing thing happens when we seek God through our trials. We come away with a deeper understanding of who He is and how much He loves us. *Overcoming faith is birthed through our struggles. As our faith is tested, the Word we have learned in our heads transforms into faith in our hearts.* This kind of faith requires tenacious prayer and great persistence. We must choose to believe His promises, even when things look hopeless, and commit our lives into the hands of a loving God. Then when the Lord directs us to do His work, we will be ready, willing, and through His strength, able.

BUILDING YOUR VISION THROUGH PRAYER

In her book, *The Prayer of Jabez for Women,* Darlene Wilkinson shares how God wants to expand our vision and influence today just as He did the woman of Proverbs 31:

> She was a woman of great influence and used her talents to serve people near and far, *yet her husband and her family remained her first priority.* We're told in verses 12 and 27, "She does [her husband] good. . . . She looks well to the ways of her household."[1]

As we consider the ways in which God will expand our vision and influence, let's remember that our lives will stay in balance only as we keep our family relationships strong.

Read Proverbs 29:18.

What does it mean to have vision or a revelation?

_____

_____

Why is it so important to seek God for His vision for your future?

_____

_____

When we have a vision from God, we have some understanding, although limited, of what God wants us to do. Through eyes of faith, we are given a greater grasp of His specific plans for us, and we are then enabled to be more focused and fruitful in the things of God. Without a vision, we have nothing restraining us to keep us from becoming sidetracked. (Not that any of us would ever get sidetracked!)

I picture running with a vision as a racehorse charging full-steam down his lane. The blinders that block his peripheral vision are there to help him focus on his target. They _restrain_ him from becoming distracted and losing the race. The same is true with us. Understanding God's vision for our lives _restrains_ us from chasing after things that would waste our time and energy.

The ironic thing to remember is that God's will for us isn't even really about us! Pastor Mark Balmer explains it this way:

> God's will is never focused on us; it's always about God. His will is that
> none should perish and that we be changed into the image of Christ.[2]

Read Habakkuk 2:2–3.

What promises and instructions are included in this passage? How do these verses encourage you in what you sense God wants to do in your life?

_____

_____

Throughout history, God has powerfully carried out His will through the lives of ordinary people just like you and me. These people had *vision.* They realized that if they would submit themselves completely to God, they could become instruments in His hands. They chose to rise above their doubt and disbelief, and instead to put their faith in the almighty God. And without exception, God honored their faith!

MARY AND ABRAHAM DID IT RIGHT!

Let's look at two people who held on to their visions from God: Mary and Abraham.

MARY

Although God's word to Mary, the mother of Jesus, came through an angel, it still had to be incredibly hard for her to fathom. She was still a virgin, yet she was to carry the Son of God in her womb. This was God's plan for this young girl, probably still in her teens. She was destined to become the mother of God. Talk about needing faith!

Read Luke 1:26–45.
What promise did God give to Mary in verse 37, and how did He confirm it to her (verses 42–44)?

_____

_____

_____

What was her response?

_____

What qualities had to be present in her life for her to respond this way?

_____

How does verse 45 speak to you about your own life?

_____

_____

_____

_____

_____

The revelation of what God wants to do in our lives doesn't usually come through an angel! More often than not His plans are revealed to us little by little as we're in prayer, in worship, or studying His Word. God gradually unfolds the next step of His plan before us, but only as we're obediently following His current instructions. Often He won't show us Step B until we're being faithful with Step A!

If you're experiencing a lack of clear direction, think back to the last thing you knew that God wanted you to do. Are you being fully obedient to everything you know He wants you to be doing? If not, you need to ask His forgiveness, and then begin to carry out the direction He's already given you.

Sin will also hinder our ability to hear and distinguish God's voice. We need to be living within His moral will for us, presented in the Ten Commandments and throughout Scripture, before we can expect to hear God's specific will for our lives.

God's Word promises to be a *lamp unto our feet* (Psalm 119:105 KJV), not a floodlight! This "lamp" often gives us just enough light to show us the next step on our path. We probably won't see the big picture all at once (it might blow us away!), but over time, the pieces of our vision will start to fit together like a puzzle. *Our part is to listen, receive His instructions, take hold of them through faith in **God's** ability, and then just do it!*

God's direction for our lives will always have these two components:

*1. It will **never** go against His Word.* In other words, God's not going to tell you to marry your pastor if you're already married! You'd be amazed at some of the crazy things people think God's telling them when they drift away from His Word. The Holy Spirit — who inspired the Bible — will not contradict Himself when He speaks to our hearts! His Word will *confirm,* never contradict, what God wants us to do.

*2. It will **always** involve fulfilling the Great Commission,* for Christ's whole purpose in coming to earth was to seek and save those who are lost (see Luke 19:10). Now don't go crazy and start packing your bags for Africa! God has not called everyone to be a missionary overseas, but *whatever God calls you to do can be used as an avenue to share your love of Christ with others.* Second Timothy 4:5 confirms this principle: *Do the work of an evangelist, fulfill your ministry* (NASB). God's heart for the lost will permeate whatever He calls us to do.

ABRAHAM

Read Romans 4:17–21.

What had God promised Abraham?

_____

_____

What two factors (see verse 19) could have caused him to doubt this vision?

_____

According to verse 20, what four things did Abraham choose to do to nurture this vision?

_____

_____

According to verse 21, when he did this, what was the outcome?

_____

_____

God gave Abraham what seemed to be an impossible vision; yet *when Abraham chose to believe Him, God did a miracle in his life.* The book of Hebrews tells us that *without faith it is impossible to please God* (11:6). That's what this whole Christian life is about: just trusting God to work His will in our lives.

He speaks.
We pray.
He answers.
We're shocked! (Don't feel bad — the disciples reacted the same way!)

Read Jeremiah 33:3 and Ephesians 3:20.
What is the common thread in these two passages of scripture?

_____

_____

_____

_____

_____

What do they imply about our prayer life, and about what God desires to do through us?

_____

_____

Our efforts to live according to God's specific plan for us can be hindered by many things. The book of Hebrews gives us some insight both into how to avoid these encumbrances and how to pray more effectively.

Read Hebrews 12:1–3.
According to verse 1, what two things are we instructed to lay aside?

_____

_____

What can we learn about "running our race" from this passage?

_____

_____

Which of these lessons encourages you?

_____

_____

EXPERIENCING GOD'S POWER THROUGH PRAYER

God is such an awesome God! To be reminded of that, all we have to do is watch a dramatic thunderstorm or attempt to count the stars. As believers, we are invited to experience His power: the power to say no to sin, the power to witness, the power to pray against the schemes of the enemy, the power to accomplish "more than we could ever ask or think" through His strength (see Ephesians 3:20).

Although many of us live far beneath all that God desires for us, some people go to the other extreme, setting the goal for their lives as nothing less than "the spectacular." The Bible teaches that God is patient toward us, _not wanting anyone to perish, but everyone to come to repentance_ (2 Peter 3:9). His ultimate "goal," if you will, is to see the lost saved — by using whatever means He sees fit. _Sometimes He uses the spectacular, but more often He uses the supernaturally natural._

But here's a warning: It's never about the power. Instead, it's always about exalting Jesus Christ. No matter how God chooses to use us, or use any ministry for that matter, the glory always belongs to Him. His Word tells us that *Jesus Christ is the same yesterday and today and forever* (Hebrews 13:8), and He is every bit as much the Miracle Worker today as He was in Bible days. And just for the record, *one soul getting saved is "spectacular," no matter how it happens!*

Read James 5:16–18.
According to the last part of verse 16, what can we count on when we pray?

_____

_____

What can we learn about Elijah from this passage? What made his prayers so effective?

_____

_____

_____

The book of 1 Kings recounts many dramatic answers to prayer that God used to reveal Himself to a lost people. Generation after generation had done evil in God's sight, serving man-made gods and worshiping idols. Eventually it came time for a showdown.

In one corner of the ring stood people from all over Israel, including 450 false prophets of Baal and 400 false prophets of Asherah. In the other corner stood lonely little Elijah. Although he stood alone, he had all the power of God behind him. From all outward appearances, the odds were stacked heavily against him. Let's see what prayer did for Elijah, keeping in mind that the Bible says he was a man just like us.

Read 1 Kings 18:20–39.
What did Elijah do in this passage?

_____

_____

According to verses 21 and 36, what were four reasons Elijah did this?

_____

_____

According to verse 39, what was the result of Elijah's bold prayer?

_____

_____

Elijah must have experienced great fear during this time. How do you conquer your own fears when you step out in faith?

_____

_____

_____

Elijah was an ordinary man who put his faith in an extraordinary God! He had grasped the crucial concept: *It's always about God! It's never about us,* so he took a huge step of faith . . . and God showed up!

Notice also that Elijah did all this at *God's command.* He didn't do it as a promotional stunt to draw crowds. It wasn't staged for a television production, designed to lure generous givers. *God chose to demonstrate His power so that the people would know that He was the one true God.* The purpose was to win their stubborn hearts and save them from sure destruction without Him. Once again, God's will is always about saving the lost, never about putting on a show.

THE ROLE OF THE HOLY SPIRIT IN PRAYER

Consider the disciples for a moment. They had walked with Jesus for three years. They were sold-out, on-fire believers. They'd been water baptized. They'd seen and even *performed* miracles. *But in Jesus' last few moments on earth, He told them about one more thing that was crucial for them to carry on His ministry.*

Read Acts 1:4–8.
According to verse 4, what were Jesus' final instructions to the disciples before He ascended into heaven?

_____

_____

_____

According to verse 8, why were these instructions given?

_____

_____

Who was the source of this power, and why was it necessary?

_____

_____

Read John 14:15–31; 15:5; 16:6–14; Acts 2:38–39; and Matthew 3:16–17.
According to John 15:5, what major problem did the disciples face now that Jesus
was about to leave the earth?

_____

_____

What was God's solution to this problem given in John 14?

_____

_____

What does John 16:7 say about the Holy Spirit's role in our lives?

_____

_____

According to John 16:13, how did Jesus say the Holy Spirit would help His
disciples?

_____

_____

According to Acts 2, who was eligible to receive the Holy Spirit?

_____

_____

If Jesus needed to be filled with the Spirit to do His work, how much more do you and
I need His power? The Holy Spirit is our wonderful gift, available to "whosoever will"
partake of Him.

PRAYER AS A LIFESTYLE

These three elements of prayer — building a relationship with God, having God's vision for our lives, and experiencing God's power — are part of God's plan for every believer. All three come about only through prayer. *Isn't it amazing how so much hinges on so little?*

As career women, wives, and mothers, all of us know too well how our prayer time can disappear, sucked into the "black hole" of our busy schedules. But we must learn to recognize that our time alone with God is especially precious, even if it requires us to stay up a little later, or to get up before the rest of the family. It will take some effort and planning, but if you'll pay the price, you'll be rewarded with a new sense of direction and stability in your life. Your time with God will become your lifeline!

God wants to do awesome things in our lives. He wants to take us on an adventure that will last a lifetime! He wants to mold us into His image, to strengthen our weaknesses, and to save us a spot next to Him on the roller coaster of Extreme Faith. But it all starts with an active prayer life.

So, what do you say? Buckle up, and let's go for it!

PRAYER

Lord, I am humbled and challenged by Your mighty power. My heart is so grateful that You care so much about me and about my every need. Thank You for the countless prayers You've answered for me over the years. Teach me to pray, Lord, and fill me with Your Holy Spirit and power. In Jesus' name. Amen.

SUMMARY POINTS

• Our prayer life is where a balanced life begins.
• We can deepen our relationship with God, discover His plan for us, and experience His power as we make prayer a priority.
• With prayer, so *much* hinges on so *little*.

FROM PRINT TO POWER: PERSONAL APPLICATION

1. In your prayer journal, describe your prayer time lately. Has it been rushed or refreshing? Was there an idea mentioned in this chapter you feel could help you? If so, write it down, and set a goal for yourself to put it into practice this week.

2. Take a few minutes to think about your understanding of God's vision for your life, including what you feel He wants you to be and accomplish. Don't limit God! All barriers aside, be it a ministry or a project, what do you feel God would have you to do?

a. Now, what is stopping you? Do you believe God is powerful enough to accomplish these goals despite the obstacles? How would it glorify God if you were able to accomplish these things?

b. List some factors that would have to change in your life for this vision to become a reality. Do you want it badly enough to make the necessary adjustments? If this vision is something that you feel is to take place in the future, are there ways you could be preparing for it now?

3. As you read in the Scripture about God's power working in ordinary lives, did it challenge you to become bolder in your prayers or your witness? Meditate on how God could work through the boldness you display in your life.

FOR FURTHER STUDY (OPTIONAL)

KEYS TO GETTING YOUR PRAYERS ANSWERED

Find the "key" given in each scripture passage below.

SCRIPTURE	KEY
1. John 15:1–7	_____
2. Matthew 6:6	_____
3. Psalm 66:18	_____
4. Matthew 21:22–23	_____
5. 1 John 5:14–15	_____
6. 1 John 3:22	_____
7. Matthew 6:14–15	_____
8. Matthew 6:7–8	_____
9. Luke 18:10–14	_____
10. Luke 18:1–8	_____
11. James 1:5–8	_____
12. 1 Thessalonians 5:17	_____
13. Colossians 4:2	_____
14. Hebrews 4:15–16	_____
15. Romans 8:26–27	_____
16. Acts 13:2–3	_____

PRAYERS FOR SPECIFIC NEEDS

The following is a list of topics with scripture passages that you can use in your prayers for specific needs.

TOPIC	SCRIPTURE
1. Salvation	Romans 10:9–10
2. Healing	James 5:14–16
3. Peace of mind	Philippians 4:6–7
4. Forgiveness	1 John 1:9
5. Willpower	Mark 14:32–38
6. For the lost	Romans 5:8–9
7. Doubt	Mark 9:24
8. Vision	Ephesians 3:14–21
9. Direction	Psalm 25:4–5
10. Deliverance	Matthew 17:14–21
11. Temptation	Luke 22:40–44
12. How to pray	Matthew 6:9–13
13. Assurance	Psalm 139

CHAPTER 6

WHEN ALL ELSE FAILS, READ THE DIRECTIONS: GETTING BACK TO THE BIBLE

"Direct me in the path of your commands, for there I find delight."
— Psalm 119:35

Picture this: You're going through life as a Christian. You love God, you attend church regularly, you love your family, and you're usually nice to those around you. But when you look around your church, you see so many other Christians who seem to have a richer depth in their walk with God than you do. You wonder how they manage to stay so strong, or if God could ever use you like He seems to be using them. What's their secret? Is there something special that sets them apart? Has God specially picked them for a closer walk with Him, or could it be just their personality?

Obviously there are many reasons why people are the way they are, and why they relate to God in different ways. But I believe that in the lives of truly strong believers, there is one constant factor: They spend time in God's Word every day. Why does that make such a difference? Because we have this promise: *"If you abide in Me, **and My words abide in you**, ask whatever you wish, and it shall be done for you"* (John 15:7 NASB). That's why!

The enemy will do anything he can to drive a wedge between you and the Word of God. He knows that if Christians get in the habit of studying the Bible on a daily basis, they will never be the same! They'll find power over their flesh and over his lies. They'll have power to live as Christ's disciples, and they'll discover God's plan for their lives.

Satan's whole scheme for our downfall can be shut down by the simple habit of reading the Scriptures daily, and applying them to our lives. You can be sure he'll do whatever it takes to keep it from happening. So he tries to tell us we're too busy, that it's a waste of time, or that the Bible is too hard to understand. He surrounds us with distractions and causes our minds to wander, or he blinds us from the love that pours out through its pages, all along trying to convince us that God is somehow against us. Never forget that the Bible calls him the father of lies!

The Bible is an amazing Book — in one volume it contains everything we need for life. It speaks to every facet of our lives, with concrete answers for some things and biblical principles for the rest . . . *if* we know how to find them. Granted, it won't tell us specifically which house to buy, or which man to marry, but God's principles can point us in the right direction and help us make godly decisions. His Word is our divine instruction manual, furnished to us "factory direct" from our Manufacturer! All we have to do is to ask Him to speak to us every time we open it, and then follow His directions!

In this chapter we will discuss various ways to study the Bible and how to get the most from our efforts when we do. We'll look at various attributes of Scripture, how it changes us, and how to apply what we learn to our busy lives. So get those pencils and Bibles ready! We're about to take a walk through God's Word.

Before we begin, share about a time when reading God's Word gave you the specific answer you needed, or about how a habit of daily Bible reading has changed your life in some way.

_____

_____

_____

_____

_____

Do you notice any difference in your spiritual strength and zeal when you faithfully spend time in the Word compared to times when you don't?

_____

_____

_____

_____

WHAT THE BIBLE SAYS ABOUT ITSELF

Read each passage and record the attributes and uses it describes.

PASSAGE	ATTRIBUTES/USES
2 Timothy 3:16–17	_____
Psalm 119:160	_____
Psalm 119:105	_____

If you truly believe what the Bible says about itself, then what is it that keeps you from absorbing it cover to cover? What distractions hinder you from studying it more thoroughly?

_____

_____

_____

If you're like me, there's just never enough time to go around! Even so, studying God's Word is worth squeezing into our busy days. But it takes *discipline.* As you sit down to read, ask God to give you understanding and to show you how the passage you're reading applies to your life. As D. L. Moody once said, "The scriptures were not given to increase our knowledge, but to change our lives."[1]

HOW READING THE WORD CAN BENEFIT YOUR LIFE

Read the following passages of scripture and list the promise given in each.

PASSAGE	PROMISE
Psalm 119:9	_____
Psalm 119:98–100	_____
Psalm 119:165	_____

Which of these rewards and promises encourage you regarding a specific need in your life right now?

_____

_____

_____

I've heard it said that lukewarm Christians have too much of the *world* in them to be happy as Christians, but too much of *Christ* in them to be happy in the world! That is a no man's land. With that in mind, one of the benefits of reading God's Word stands out from the rest: *simply knowing Him.*

Our fellowship will be sweeter as we know and understand God better. Our consciences will be clear, and we'll have peace with Him and with others. When we make God's Word a priority in our lives, we experience His blessings, His direction, and His encouragement. Most of all, we are continually reminded of His awesome love toward us. And that relationship, my friend, is what life's all about!

How God's Word Changes Us

1. God's Word Changes Our Thinking.

Reading the Bible is just like making a deposit in our spiritual savings account. When we need its answers or guidance, we can draw out only what we've already put in! And although we may not be able to spend hours each day making "deposits," our twenty minutes here and ten minutes there will add up like a reservoir of strength and wisdom to which we can turn when it's needed.

Read Romans 12:1–2.
Since verse 2 doesn't tell us to "transform ourselves," how will change take place? Provide examples of what might change in your life when you begin to read the Bible with regularity.

_____

_____

_____

_____

_____

We *allow* ourselves to be changed by the renewing of our minds *as we read the Word.* We *choose* to subject our lives to what we read. This transformation must be personal! *Rather than taking it in one ear and letting it go out the other, we must choose to take each passage to heart, meditate on it, and ask the Lord how its principles apply to our own lives.* Then God's Word can move from our heads to our hearts, and our actions will begin to follow!

2. GOD'S WORD HELPS US MAKE GODLY DECISIONS.

I must be missing a decision-making gene of some sort, because I'm the worst when it comes to making a final choice! Just ask anyone who's ever gone out to eat with me. I always have to order last, because I want to hear what everyone else is having before I decide! And when it comes to buying Christmas gifts . . . I always end up waiting until the last minute *because I just can't make up my mind.*

Of course what I eat doesn't make much difference in the grand scheme of things (except on my bathroom scale!) And the Christmas presents usually do end up under the tree just in time. Those things are temporary. It's the daily decisions that affect our families and determine our fruitfulness for God which chart the course of our lives, for better or worse. How can we choose what's best? Can we trust our feelings? What about when our minds tell us one thing and our hearts tell us another? Is there a way to distinguish God's will from our own thoughts? Let's see what we can learn about this from the Master.

Read Matthew 4:1–10.

While Jesus was on earth, how did He make His decisions?

_____

How does His example challenge you?

_____

_____

Read 1 Thessalonians 5:23 and Hebrews 4:12.

According to 1 Thessalonians, man is made up of what three elements?

_____

In Hebrews 4:12, what characteristics of the Bible are described?

_____

_____

Distinguishing which of our thoughts are from ourselves and which are from God may be one of the most valuable benefits of knowing God's Word. Our souls are made up of our mind, will, and emotions. They represent our flesh or "natural man."

In contrast, our spirit is our inner man — the heart of who we are. The spirit is the part of us that can hear and respond to God. Our challenge is to distinguish which is speaking to us — our minds, our own wills, our emotions, or our spirit — so we can follow the right one! As a two-edged sword, God's Word slices through our confusion, misunderstandings, and stubbornness to show us the truth. *His Word illuminates for us what's coming from God and what's coming from us, when our minds can't tell the difference.*

I picture God's Word like a coffee filter over my head, allowing God's thoughts to flow into my mind and sifting out my worldly thoughts. When I start to believe things that aren't biblical, the Holy Spirit uses the verses I've studied to wave a red flag in my face and warn me that I'm veering off track. It's like God's own emergency broadcast system right to me! The more of the Word that's inside of my mind and my spirit, the easier it becomes to recognize the difference between worldly thoughts and the prompting of the Holy Spirit. This kind of discernment can give us the clear direction and guidance we need to do the right thing when we face tough decisions in life.

In my college days, there was a time when I thought the Lord was calling me to become involved with a church that was known for its radical commitment to Christ. Despite the pull that was in my spirit, the rest of me wasn't sure that it was the right thing to do. Needless to say, I was confused.

In my *mind* I reasoned that I could still be a good Christian without being *that* committed. My stubborn *will* told me, "Nobody's going to tell me what to do!" And my *emotions* whispered, "You'll never find a decent guy to marry in that church!" Meanwhile, my *spirit* kept drawing me there, confirming this direction over and over to me.

When I turned to the Word for an answer, I was led to read Romans 1, which provides a vivid account of all the terrible things that can happen to Christians when they don't obey the Lord! I clearly had my answer!

I don't recommend just opening the Bible and pointing to one single verse as the answer for whatever it is that you're seeking. A better way is to study what you feel God is saying to you through more than one passage and ask God to confirm His Word to you. If you still need direction, get some counsel from a mature believer. *When we find ourselves torn between the many duties and concerns of the day, God's Word can cut to the heart of the matter and remind us of what's important to Him. That's the power of the Word!*

For the record, I did end up going to that church, and it brought about tremendous spiritual growth in my life. And my quest for a husband? The pastor of that church asked me to co-lead a home group with a "radical" guy named Dave Folkerts . . . and the rest is history! In fact, we just celebrated our twenty-first wedding anniversary. God knew what He was doing all along!

Share about a time when the Lord used His Word to show you the difference between *His* will and *your* own thoughts and desires. What were the results, and what did you learn from the experience?

_____

_____

_____

_____

3. GOD'S WORD PRODUCES LASTING FRUIT IN OUR LIVES.

As we grow in our relationship with God, we should begin to see positive change in our lives. These changes, sometimes known as "fruit," should be evident as we abide in the Vine, who is Jesus.

Read John 15:1–8 and Joshua 1:8.
What does it mean to "remain in the vine" (John 15:4)? What does that have to do with reading the Bible?

_____

_____

According to Joshua 1:8, what three things are we commanded to do with the Word, and what two things will be the result if we do?

_____

_____

_____

Some people have used the terms *success* and *prosperity* as the basis of a self-promoting doctrine. They've taught a prosperity doctrine as if God's principles were simply a scheme to "get rich quick." Is financial gain the primary reason we need to be able to quote God's Word? Let's let the Word of God speak for itself.

Read 1 Timothy 6:9–11 and Psalm 1:1–3.

What does this passage in 1 Timothy teach us about the desire to get rich quick?

_____

List some of the dangers of the "love of money" you see in 1 Timothy 6:9 and 10.

_____

_____

What are we instructed to focus our attention on instead of riches?

_____

Using Psalm 1:1–3 as a guide, how would you describe true prosperity?

_____

_____

WHAT HAPPENS WHEN WE NEGLECT THE WORD?

When we ignore God's Word we become dry and thirsty. If the neglect of Scripture becomes a pattern, God often allows a downward spiral to begin in our lives in order to woo us back to Himself.

As my husband, Dave, says, "God leads us into the desert to show us our need for the Living Water. Temptations will always accompany the stress in our lives, bringing us to a fork in the road. In that place, we either choose to trust God and handle it His way, or give in to the temptation to handle our problems the world's way. What we do at that point will determine our growth, or lack of it."

Read Hosea 4:6.
According to this passage, what can happen when we neglect the Word?

_____

_____

The awareness of such a severe consequence should wake us up and spur us on to study the Word for ourselves! I can't tell you how many times I've wanted to do something so badly, but the Word of God stopped me and kept me from making a huge mistake. At other times I *haven't* wanted to do something that I knew I should, and the Word has given me the power and conviction to do it anyway. *When I neglect God's Word, I'm neglecting the most powerful source of encouragement known to man!* God knows I can live my life for Him only when I get my daily dose of encouragement and direction from His Word. Without it, I'm sunk!

Read John 14:15.

Is it possible to walk in obedience to God's Word if we don't really know what it says?

_____

Have you ever thought that your commitment to the Word could be a measure of your commitment to God? If that is true, what does your attitude toward the Bible say about your love for God?

_____

_____

Read Mark 4:3–8, 13–20.

According to verses 15 through 19, even though the people mentioned had heard the Word, what things prevented it from producing fruit in their lives?

_____

_____

What was different about those people discussed in verse 20?

_____

_____

What can we learn from this story?

_____

_____

_____

Read John 8:31–32 and fill in the blanks below.

If you _____, then you are really _____.

And if you are really _____, you will know _____

and the truth will _____. (See both verses 31 and 32.)

According to verse 32, what does the knowledge of the truth do in our lives?

_____

Write out the opposite of the previous statement in the blanks below.

If you don't _____, then you really aren't _____,

and you won't _____ and the truth won't _____.

It's something to think about. We're designed to run on the fuel of God's Word, and we will quickly run out of gas without it!

FIVE WAYS TO LEARN GOD'S WORD

We've established what God's Word is, how it changes us, the benefits of reading it, and the consequences when we neglect it. But in all practicality, how can we get it off the page and into our hearts where it can make a difference? I'm so glad you asked! Let's look at several ways to get the most out of our time in the Bible.

Look up the following scripture passages and note the method of study that is described, as well as the results that method achieved.

READ	METHOD	RESULTS
Romans 10:17	_____	_____
Acts 17:11	_____	_____
Psalm 119:11	_____	_____
Psalm 119:97-99	_____	_____
James 1:22	_____	_____

Which of these methods is most effective for you, and how and when have you made time for it?

_____

_____

_____

Are there habits you have cultivated in your study time that could help others?

_____

_____

_____

As Christians, we *want* to hear from God, but so often our minds are busy stewing over problems. Our ears are full of conversations and demands. We squeeze in time to read the newspaper, but not the Bible. And our "meditations" are on the business at hand — what still remains on our to-do list as we hurry here and there, trying to balance life intellectually rather than spiritually. And we wonder why God's leading is so hard to discern...

To counteract the demanding voices of the world, there are many ways we can plant the Word in our hearts. We can *hear* the Word being taught in church, through teaching tapes, or in worship music. We can *study* it chronologically, by topic, by book, by verse, by word, or even by character. Commentaries and concordances are available in books or on software, and study Bibles with extensive outlines and background information are also a great way to enrich your understanding.

By far, scripture memorization and meditation are our best defense against the schemes of the enemy. When God reveals His truth to us personally, it acts as an anchor in the storms of life, during those times when it's easier to be led by our feelings rather than our faith. As we meditate on God's Word, it becomes an unchanging, unshakable Rock in our lives. When we memorize scripture, we fill our reservoir with the strength and stability that we have in God. Pondering what the Word says to us, and about us, is what makes the Scriptures come to life!

As busy wives and mothers, we must spend time in the Word . . . for our sanity if nothing else! Who else in this world is required to do more for more people than most women are?! *We need God's supernatural power to do all that's demanded of us* — to keep ourselves and our families organized, to do one hundred things at once, to hold our tongues when we feel like yelling, to hug instead of insulting, to be patient instead of giving up, and to hang in there when we feel like running away! God's Word keeps our heads on straight. It keeps things in perspective, sustains our joy, and renews our hope.

I don't know about you, but I call that good news!

PRAYER

Father, You know me inside and out. You know my responsibilities and the demands on my time, and yet You have commanded me to make time to study Your Word. Show me how, Lord. Help me to be diligent in my efforts and to hear Your heart so that I can understand Your direction for my daily life. Change me into the person You want me to be. I love You, Lord. In Jesus' name. Amen.

SUMMARY POINTS

• God's Word is our standard to live by.
• Reading God's Word will change our character and our lives.
• We learn God's Word by reading it, hearing it, studying it, memorizing it, meditating on it, and putting it into practice.
• When we neglect the Word, we will thirst for the Living Water.

FROM PRINT TO POWER: PERSONAL APPLICATION

1. Think about a situation or a decision in your life about which you could use some godly counsel.

2. Look over the methods of study on the next few pages and decide which would be most helpful to you in this situation or decision. For example, you could choose to do a topical study on discipline, or memorize some key scriptures on diligence.

3. Make an appointment with God for study time every day this week. Jot it down in your Daytimer, along with what you plan to study.

4. Pray about what keeps you from spending more time in the Word, and ask God to show you how to overcome it. If you simply feel too pressed for time, ask Him to show you a good time to read every day, or a better time if you're already in a schedule.

FOR FURTHER STUDY (OPTIONAL)

METHODS OF STUDYING GOD'S WORD

1. Topical Study:

a. Pick a topic.

b. In a concordance, look up all references to this topic and jot down what they say to you.

c. Look up cross-references from these verses, and record their main thoughts. (These are the little letters and numbers that are written within the verse itself, in the margins, or at the bottom of the page. They refer you to other passages that speak about similar issues. If the Bible you are using doesn't have these, borrow another version or edition from a friend).

d. In a concordance, look up some words that are opposites of the topic you have chosen; for example, for "diligence" look up "laziness." Record the main thoughts from each of these verses.

e. Ask yourself the following questions:

    1. How does this topic apply to my life?

    2. Is there a command for me to obey?

    3. Is there an instruction I need to follow?

    4. What are the benefits of abiding in the Word concerning this topic?

    5. What are the consequences if I don't?

    6. What similar truths has God revealed to me in the past?

f. Look over all that you have found. Pray, and then write a paragraph summarizing what you learned and what God showed you about the topic.

2. Word Study:

a. Select a word that you want to study.

b. With a concordance, list all of the verses that contain that particular word. If there are too many, choose the ones that stand out to you.

c. Look them up, and write down what they say to you.

d. Look up any cross-references that are included with these verses, and write what each of them is saying.

e. Read over and then pray about what you've found. Write a paragraph summarizing what you have learned and what God has shown you through this study.

3. Verse Study:

a. Pick a verse and write it down, complete with all references listed in the verse and in the margin. Write down what you feel God is saying to you about it.

b. Read the verses before and after it, and summarize the context of the writing. Is there an overall statement or point that this verse makes?

c. Rewrite the verse in your own words using different adjectives or nouns that denote the same meaning.

d. Look up all cross-references listed with the verse, and record the main thought of each.

e. Read over all that you have found, asking God to give you understanding about what you've read. Finally, write a paragraph summarizing what you've learned and what God has shown you through this study.

4. Chapter Study:

a. Choose a chapter that you would like to study. Read through it and find its main subject.

b. Give the chapter a title that summarizes its main content.

c. Outline the main thoughts of the chapter.

d. Ask the following questions:

    1. What is the key verse of this chapter?

    2. What does this chapter teach me about Jesus?

    3. Is there any sin for me to confess or forsake listed in this chapter?

    4. Is there any command for me to obey listed in this chapter?

    5. Is there any promise for me to stand on given in this chapter?

    6. Is there any instruction for me to follow given in this chapter?

    7. Is there any prayer that I should pray, according to this chapter?

e. For a more in-depth study, do a verse study on the main verse in each section of the chapter.

5. Character Study:

a. Choose a character whom you want to learn more about.

b. In a concordance, find the character, and then make a list of all the references to him or her. If there are too many, choose the ones that stand out to you.

c. Read each passage and record what is revealed about the character. You could also read whole passages of the Bible in which this person's life is prominent.

d. Ask yourself the following questions about this person:

    1. What was his/her motivation in life?

    2. What things may have hindered his/her walk with God?

    3. What were his/her strengths?

    4. How did this person handle trials or difficult situations?

    5. What are the similarities/differences between this person and myself?

    6. What qualities in this person do I desire to have in my own life?

    7. Can I tell how much time this person spent in prayer, the Word, or in fellowship with God?

    8. What can I learn from this person's walk with God?

e. Read over all that you've found. Pray, and then write a summary paragraph about what the Lord taught you through this study.

CHAPTER 7

LEARNING TO FOLLOW GOD

"Call to Me and I will answer you, and I will tell you great and mighty things, which you do not know."

— Jeremiah 33:3 NASB

Picture this: You're suddenly single again — although this time around you have three hungry mouths to feed. You have no roots to speak of. Your family is distant; friends are busy with their own problems. Your job provides a paycheck, but it's not what you want to do forever, and money is tight. Should you look for a second job, finish your degree, or pack up and move across the country to be closer to your family? How are you supposed to know what's the best thing to do?

Or consider this scenario: Your son is fourteen now, the youngest of three. While his two older sisters are doing well in school, he has other priorities. Instead of doing his homework, he'd rather play video games. You know he has the ability to do well, but nothing seems to motivate him. His grades are slipping, and you wonder how he'll ever get into college. To top it all off, you're sure his new "best friend" is bad news. What should you do?

The bottom-line common denominator in these two situations is obvious: We need answers. Direction. Wisdom. Good judgment. Even the ability to foresee the future. We need to know how to function as Christians, not only on Sundays in church, but out in the real world — where the rubber meets the road. *The bottom line is this: We need to know how to hear from God.*

TRUE ANSWERS COME THROUGH A RELATIONSHIP

Our invitation to communicate with the almighty God is what makes the difference between a religion and a relationship, between learning from the Book and being taught by the Teacher. *The answers we need can only come through a relationship with our Creator.* When this relationship is strong, we'll be encouraged as He speaks joy and courage into our weary hearts — even when life hands us more than we can bear. But that can't happen if we don't learn how to recognize His voice. In this chapter we'll take a look at how to hear God's voice and His direction, as well as how to guard our hearts from all the other "voices" that are out there!

Take a moment to jot down anything that may have caused you turmoil lately. It could be a situation, relationship, or circumstance in which you need God's wisdom.

_____

_____

_____

_____

Many Christians have the opinion that God never does and never will speak to them. But if that were true, then how did they get saved? There's only one way! The Scripture teaches that unless God draws us, we can't (or won't) ever come to Him. In other words, when we yield our lives to Him, it is in *response* to God's initial contact with us! He first *speaks* to our hearts to reveal our need for Him. If you're saved, God has spoken to you at least once!

When we make daily choices that glorify God, it's because the Holy Spirit is at work in our hearts and minds, directing us to do what's right. He is constantly communicating with us, whether or not we're listening or tuning in, because God's desire is to show us His love every day! *For God so loved* (you). . . . Finding God's will is always best achieved when we meet with Him regularly. That must be why He doesn't give us all the answers we need at once — He wants us to keep coming back for more!

Read John 10:1–15.

Jesus uses this story to describe the relationship between a loving, protective Shepherd and His sheep. List some of the characteristics of this relationship that are described in verses 3 through 5, and verse 14.

_____

_____

What can we learn about hearing God's voice through this story, and how does this encourage you?

_____

_____

_____

As we attempt to distinguish God's voice and His direction from the clamor that surrounds us, our roots must go deep in His Word. It's only there that we can truly learn to recognize His voice and discern His character. Once we study *who* He is and *how* He acts, we'll start to recognize His standards and anticipate His reactions. Couples who have been married for many years are like that. One can start a sentence and the other will finish it! God promises that as we seek Him, He will make His will known to us.

Read Jeremiah 33:3.
What promise do we find in this passage about hearing God's direction?

_____

_____

How could this apply to your life today?

_____

_____

FOCUSING ON GOD'S WILL

Hebrews 11:6 tells us that *God rewards those who earnestly seek Him.* Our ability to hear God's voice and discern His direction will take effort and discipline. It requires us to give Him three things: our attention, our worship, and ultimately our lives. But this small sacrifice on our part is worth the effort we make, because the rewards — knowing Him and His will for our lives — are out of this world!

Read Proverbs 4:20–22.

According to verses 20 and 21, there are three ways to stay open to God's leading. What are they?

_____

_____

What are some practical ways you can make these a part of your life?

_____

_____

_____

How sad it is when our busy lifestyles crowd out the very thing that would give us the direction we need to survive! *If we never slow down and be still before God, we'll never hear His voice.* Part of the solution must be to *make* time to be with God, and then *guard* it with our very lives! (Lock yourself in the bathroom if you have to!) You may need to cut out some of your activities and even lower your standards in others to make time with God a part of your daily routine. But the result will enable you to refocus the camera lens of your life and see your priorities that much more clearly.

John and Charles Wesley's mother, who had eighteen children — and lived to tell about it — made time with God by pulling her apron over her head! When her brood saw the apron go up, they knew that it meant, "Don't even *think* about bothering me right now!" Her "quiet time" with God is living proof that where there's a will, there's a way!

Read Acts 13:1–2.

What happened as the believers fasted and worshiped the Lord?

_____

_____

On the following lines, share about a time when you felt God give you direction as you worshiped Him.

_____

_____

_____

_____

_____

When the disciples made finding God's will their number-one priority, He made it clear to them. Notice they *didn't* say, "Here's our plan, Lord; please bless it." They wanted to find out *God's* plan, and as they exalted Him through their worship, He revealed it to them. They weren't seeking His hand — they were seeking His face. Big difference! *In true worship, our hearts yield to Him in a way that says, "Whatever You want, Lord. I'm Yours."*

Galatians 2:20 reads, *I have been crucified with Christ; and it is no longer I who live, but Christ lives in me* (NASB). There's that yielded heart again! When we're not our own — *when we're not in charge* — it makes sense that God would lead us. The person in the casket doesn't demand his own way — he's dead! He doesn't try to tell the mortician what to do with him. In the same way, *when we're not grasping for our way, or bucking against God's will, hearing God's direction becomes a whole lot easier.* We simply trust and obey, one step at a time, and let God figure out the details. Life becomes so much easier when we do!

How God Directs Us

Let's take a look at the various ways that God uses to direct His children.

1. God Directs Us through His Word.

The number-one way to determine the will of God for our lives is to immerse ourselves in His Word. That makes sense, doesn't it? If the Word says, "Thou shalt not," then thou shalt not! Some aspects of the will of God become fairly obvious when we open up the pages of the Bible, and it doesn't take a rocket scientist to figure them out. For example, because the Word tells us, *Love your neighbor,* we can know that anything God calls us to do will not contradict that directive. So much of the daily direction that we seek is already spelled out in simple terms in the Bible — God's will for every Christian. Most of us would have our hands full just doing that!

Obviously, however, many of the more specific questions that we have aren't answered in such a black-and-white way. But in order to recognize God's voice in these situations, we must first learn to recognize it in Scripture as He speaks to our hearts while we read.

The written Word is our "plumb line," our standard, for truth. *Every tiny bit of direction we receive **that is truly from God, will always line up with the Word,*** no matter from whom or where else it comes. In these days when it seems as if anything goes, God's Word is our safety net that will keep us from falling for ungodly direction. God's Word is His voice, and the two are inseparable.

The Bible is the only *living* book ever written, because a *living* God speaks through it to His people. If that's true, what happens when it's no longer directly in front of us? Do we simply hope we've "stored up" enough of its information in the morning to last us through the day? And what if what we read earlier doesn't pertain to the situation we find ourselves in later? Are we, so to speak, out of luck?!

Certainly not! God will remind us of what He has shown us earlier as we've studied His Word, and that same still, small voice we've come to recognize when we read the Bible will continue to direct us with His truths throughout the day.

Read Isaiah 55:8–9.
According to these verses, why is it so important to know the difference between God's will and our own opinions?

_____

_____

Share about a time when you experienced this truth.

_____

_____

_____

_____

Sometimes God directs us through His Word by showing us the possible consequences of our actions. For example, the children of Israel continually complained, lost hope, and worshiped other gods, all of which frequently caused them to miss God's best. Bible stories of both godly and ungodly characters can alert us to disaster and keep us motivated to do what God says.

We learn God's direction for us as we read about His attitude toward sin — and toward sinners. We see how Jesus reacted in kindness to the woman caught in adultery, how He denounced the Pharisees for their hypocrisy, and how He took time to share His love and affection with children. Because we know He is the same yesterday, today, and forever, we can know how He must feel about similar situations in our lives today.

Simply put, God uses His Word to speak to us — right in the middle of the circumstances of our lives. When we receive Christ as our Savior, the Holy Spirit comes to live within us. Then, as we read His Word, He bears witness to the truth of the Scriptures and how it applies to our own lives. *God's spoken word to us gives life to His written Word, **adapting it to our individual situations.*** Our part is to mix that word with faith, choosing to believe that God is able to make what He says a reality in our lives, no matter how impossible it might seem.

2. GOD DIRECTS US THROUGH HIS CHURCH AND OTHER BELIEVERS.

A second way in which God intends for us to receive godly direction is through His bride, the church — both from the pulpit and echoed in the words of mature believers. Committing ourselves to a church where God's Word is central, and where we can learn to serve others is a vital aspect of learning to hear from God. Our part is to arrive at church "prayed up" and prepared, ready to obey what we're taught. God places each one in the body of Christ as He wills, to nurture, encourage, and keep each other focused on living for Christ.

Read Ephesians 4:11–13 and Hebrews 10:24–25.
According to Ephesians 4:11, what five offices of ministry has God placed within His church?

_____

_____

In verses 12 and 13, what are the four reasons these offices are given?

_____

_____

From Hebrews 10, why is it so important that Christians commit to being active in a local church?

_____

_____

How has being committed to a body of believers blessed your own life?

_____

_____

The five-fold ministry spoken of in Ephesians has been set apart by God to equip the rest of us for service, not necessarily for these ministers to do everything all by themselves. So many of us have had this crazy idea that "ministry" is only supposed to happen through those church workers who get paid for it! But this passage says that the true task of these ministers is to help *us* become fit and ready to work for God — our own "personal trainers," if you will.

Don't neglect becoming involved in a church. You'll miss out on so much of what God wants to do in your life if you insist on being a Lone Ranger! And remember — being active in church is as much about giving as it is receiving.

3. God Speaks in a Still, Small Voice.

Time spent in the Word, in prayer, in being taught by those in ministry, and in fellowship with other believers works together to lay a firm foundation for our faith. With every brick of this foundation in place, we open the door to hearing that still, small voice within us, as the almighty God chooses to reveal Himself to us.

Learning to hear and recognize God's voice has been a priceless treasure to me. God will speak something to my heart, and confirm it in His Word or through other believers, and soon I know for certain it's His will for me. And *when I know it's His will, I know it's His best!* Hearing from God takes the guesswork out of life. He leads. We follow. We're blessed!

This communication happens through the Holy Spirit within us. His presence in us is our connection to God, almost like an internal satellite dish that picks up transmissions from God's heart. Talk about wireless communication! Let's take a look at some promises that will help us discern God's direction for our lives.

Read John 14:16–17, 26 and John 16:13.
According to John 14:17, where is the Holy Spirit active in a believer's life?

_____

_____

From John 14:26, what two things did Jesus say the Holy Spirit would do for us?

_____

_____

And in John 16:13, what three things did He promise to do?

_____

_____

How can these things help us understand how God is directing us?

_____

_____

_____

Note that the Holy Spirit speaks, not of His own initiative, but only what He hears from God. How can we hear from God? We hear through the Holy Spirit! When Jesus returned to heaven, the Father sent the Holy Spirit to be God's voice on earth. Now God speaks to each of us as individuals through the Holy Spirit, just as Jesus spoke to His disciples face to face. *So whether the words came through Jesus while on earth, or now through the Holy Spirit, they are still God's words!*

Our part, then, is to listen closely for His direction, recognize His voice from among all the other voices that surround us, and then diligently follow His guidance. When we do, God will bless our obedience.

Read Romans 8:14 and 1 Corinthians 2:6–12.
According to these passages of scripture, how can Christians discover God's will?

_____

_____

Summarize what these verses speak to you about your own life.

_____

_____

_____

4. GOD DIRECTS US THROUGH THE PROMPTING OF THE HOLY SPIRIT.

The prompting of the Holy Spirit is a bit hard to explain. It is often like knowing something without being told. We may not literally hear God's *words* to us, but we understand His *heart.* It's like a green light inside of us, telling us that God wants us to do something, or it can be like a red flag warning us that something's not right.

In some ways, the prompting of the Holy Spirit is like a courtroom, where a witness gives a testimony of what he knows, for or against the defendant. In the same way, the Holy Spirit inside of us bears witness for or against whatever is in question. He leads us toward some things, and away from others, always according to the Father's will.

Read Acts 20:22–23.

In this scripture passage, the apostle Paul was both compelled by the Spirit and warned by Him about what was ahead. Have you ever experienced a prompting to do something, or a warning to *not* do something? Explain.

_____

_____

_____

How did you know the prompting was from God?

_____

_____

At times, the thing you're considering may at first seem to be logical and inviting, but the Holy Spirit will prompt you to do otherwise, even when you don't understand why. This is when we're called to *walk by faith and not by sight* as it is described in 2 Corinthians 5:7 (NASB).

As I mentioned in an earlier chapter, this is what we experienced when God stirred our hearts to move south, even though at the time it didn't seem to make sense. We had a fruitful ministry where we lived, but after much time seeking God through prayer and the Word, we felt the Holy Spirit *compelling* us to move to Florida for some unknown reason.

Only God knew how the move would open up a door for Dave to enter the full-time ministry and allow us to touch many more lives than if we'd stayed. We walked solely by faith (since we didn't have a clue why we were moving), trusting the leading of the Holy Spirit, and it's been the best thing we've ever done!

This prompting of the Holy Spirit is different than mere feelings or emotions. Feelings are fickle and unreliable. They come from our flesh, and can change according to our moods and circumstances. In contrast, *the Holy Spirit's prompting remains constant and unchanging.* God's Word says that the Holy Spirit will lead us into all truth. It is 100 percent reliable when we discern it accurately. That's the tricky part!

Read Colossians 3:15.

Which "fruit of the Spirit" should we sense when God is leading us?

_____

How have you experienced this particular leading in your own life?

_____
_____
_____
_____

When we find ourselves torn between two options, unsure about which is the right thing to do, we can let *the peace of God* be our judge, that is, the deciding factor about whether or not we're in His will. When we're out of God's will, we simply won't have the peace of God. Put it this way: If there's turmoil in your heart about something you're about to do, then don't do it! On the other hand, if you're convinced that you're in God's will, you can let that peace rule in your heart over and above worry and doubt, trusting that because it's God's will, everything will work out for the best.

Likewise, God doesn't usually drive us to do things, forcing us to make quick decisions. I've heard it said that Satan pushes, but the Holy Spirit gently tugs. When that happens, we're motivated by compassion, not manipulated by compulsion. What a difference!

5. GOD DIRECTS US THROUGH CIRCUMSTANCES.
I believe that God uses circumstances to prepare us for change or to push us out of our comfort zones. Yet relying solely on circumstances, on open and closed doors, can be risky. Some doors are meant to be opened through prayer, as we see when Daniel prayed for twenty-one days to receive his answer. Other times we may kick those doors open like a SWAT team member, only to find ourselves hurting, and we think, *I guess I just can't trust God.* No, that wasn't God. That was your foot!

King David could have said he had an "open door" to take advantage of Bathsheba when he spotted her bathing from his rooftop. The circumstances lined up: Her hubby was away at war (where David should have been), and she needed someone to keep her company. . . . But was this open door from God? No way! That one sin led to the murder of Bathsheba's husband, the birth of an illegitimate child, and David living in sin for a full year before he repented. God doesn't open doors for us to sin!

The same thing could have been said about Jonah as he boarded the get-away boat when God had clearly called him to Nineveh. Jonah was at the dock, and there sat a boat, ready and waiting to take him to Tarshish. The circumstances might seem to indicate an "open door" to go in that direction, but was it from God? Not on your life!

On the other hand, when Moses saw the burning bush, it was an open door from God. It was Moses' call to the ministry, and God was very much involved in the situation. The only reliable way to distinguish which is a truly open door and which is a temptation is to be full of the Word of God.

DISTINGUISHING GOD'S VOICE FROM THE VOICES OF SATAN OR SELF

While we learn to follow God's direction, there will be times when we hear more than one voice. We know that Eve heard two voices, and when she stopped listening to God and started listening to Satan, her problems began. The same can be true for us. That's why it's so crucial for us to learn to recognize the difference between what comes from our flesh, what comes from Satan, and what comes from God. We can get into some terrible messes when we don't seek God for His direction, and instead trust in our own intelligence to lead us. Take it from me. You always end up learning the hard way!

Let's look to the Word to discover some ways in which we can learn to hear the voice of the Lord.

Read the following scripture passages and list the methods God uses to get His message through to His people.

VERSE	METHOD(S) USED
Isaiah 30:21	_____
1 Samuel 3:1–10	_____
Romans 8:14	_____
Genesis 37:5–9	_____
Proverbs 15:22	_____
1 Corinthians 12:4–8	_____

Has the Lord ever used any of these methods to speak to you? If so, explain the situation.

_____

_____

_____

_____

_____

_____

What convinced you it was God speaking, and how did His direction help you in your situation?

_____

_____

_____

_____

Before we accept any direction as coming from God, we must first judge it according to the Word. Does it line up with the principles God has already given us? Will it cause your faith to grow, or will it cause you to doubt God's Word? Does your spirit bear witness with it? Does it confirm something that God has already spoken to you?

This may take some time. When God speaks to our hearts, often He just shows us a little piece of the puzzle for us to act on immediately, or to build a bigger picture of what He wants to do in our future. Once we've prayed, we can respond in one of three ways: (1) Receive the direction as coming from God, (2) dismiss it as coming from ourselves, or (3) reject it as a lie coming from the enemy.

This discernment requires much caution and care, because much of what circulates among Christians as truth doesn't always line up with God's Word. Well-meaning people mix Scripture with worldly wisdom and allow it to direct their lives as if it were gospel truth. That's so dangerous! It may _sound_ spiritual, but if it's not God's specific word to us, it could lead us astray. _We're commanded to run the race marked out **for us**, not for someone else!_ (See Hebrews 12:1.) We can become sidetracked when we try to follow the popular opinion, simply because we haven't taken time to hear God's specific instructions to us as individuals!

WHAT IF WE'RE NOT SURE WHAT TO DO?

Instead of telling us everything all at once, God teaches us to walk by faith, allowing that faith to mature as we learn to trust Him in all our circumstances. At some time in our lives, we will all go through situations when we just don't know what to do. Almost without exception, the faith of the men and women we look up to as spiritual leaders have gone through some time in the "desert," as their faith has been tested. *During those dry times, God turns our tests into testimonies, as our roots go deep in Him.* It's during trials that His Word truly becomes our hope and comfort.

Read James 1:5, 22.

What are we instructed to do when we need God's wisdom?

_____

_____

According to verse 22, what can hinder us from getting further direction from God?

_____

_____

_____

When we just can't seem to hear God's voice, we need to make sure our hearts are clean. If we're living in sin, we can't expect to hear from Him, for Psalm 66:18 tells us, *If I had cherished sin in my heart, the Lord would not have listened.* Our ability to discern God's direction will be directly hindered by disobedience, rebellion, entanglement with the worries of the world, resistance to change, yielding to fear, being carnally minded, or simply failing to spend time with Him. If you realize that you've blown it, confess your sin to God, and 1 John 1:9 promises that He'll forgive you.

If you've done all that you know to do and you don't know what to do next, then go back to what you know about God. He's in control and has promised to lead you. Be patient, be faithful, stay in His Word, and keep waiting!

How Our Lives Will Change
As We Hear and Obey

As we seek God in worship, prayer, and the study of His Word, our lives will become more focused and fruitful. We'll experience a keener sense of His purpose and direction, and we'll become more efficient with our time, wasting less and spending more on the important things in life. Decision-making will become less a matter of weighing all of our options, and more a matter of hearing from the "Wonderful Counselor." *Best of all, our walk with God will become the treasure of our lives.* The peace that comes from knowing God is in control of the details of our lives is priceless. Let's do what it takes to live in it every day!

Prayer

Lord, my heart's desire is to know You. I ask that You take what I have read and learned today and mold it into my daily life. Holy Spirit, please teach me how to hear Your voice and follow Your leading. Help me to obey You so that my life will bring glory to Your name. In Jesus' name I pray. Amen.

Summary Points

• The answers we need for life come through an ongoing relationship with God.

• God directs us through His Word, the church, other believers, His voice, circumstances, and the prompting of the Holy Spirit.

• Being led by circumstances alone is risky.

• Our lives will change as we listen to Him and obey His direction.

From Print to Power: Personal Application

1. Think about your walk with Christ. Are you currently hearing His voice? Do you sense His leading? If so, what helps you discern His voice from the other voices in your life?

_____

_____

_____

_____

_____

2. Earlier in this chapter I asked you to jot down some situations in which you need direction at this time. What did you learn in our study that could help you hear God's direction concerning these circumstances?

_____

_____

_____

_____

_____

3. As you read about giving God your attention, your worship, and your life, did one or more of these "ring a bell" with you? Are there any changes you feel that you should make that could strengthen your relationship with God? Write down your thoughts and pray about how to integrate these changes into your schedule this week.

_____

_____

_____

_____

_____

_____

_____

_____

CHAPTER 8

GOD'S BLUEPRINT FOR MARRIAGE

"A cord of three strands is not quickly broken."
— Ecclesiastes 4:12

Imagine, if you will, that you and your husband have been tucking away money for years, and you finally set out to build your dream home. You select a blueprint, choose a builder, and begin to lay out the big bucks necessary to make your dream a reality. You just know it's going to be great!

But when the construction crew arrives, something is very wrong. One guy starts to dig the hole on one side of the site; another guy shows up to put on the roof; and a third guy decides to build a ranch instead of a two-story! What in the world is happening?

Immediately you shout, "Everybody just stop! Where's the general contractor? Who's in charge here, and where's our blueprint? You guys desperately need some direction here, or this whole thing is going be a disaster — *and I'm paying for it!"*

The need for a leader in a building project like this should be obvious to most of us, but how often do we attempt the much bigger project of a lasting marriage — "until death do us part" — without a clue as to what we're doing? We pay a fortune for the wedding, but then when challenges come our way that test our commitment, we don't know what to do. We struggle to determine who's in charge, and then desperately search for a counselor to help us.

I have both good news and bad news for you. The good news is there is a Master Builder who has a perfect, customized blueprint for your marriage. Great! The bad news is . . . you're not Him! But relax — neither is your husband! Let's take a look at who the Bible says is supposed to be in charge.

Read Psalm 127:1.

According to this verse, who should ultimately be in charge of our marriage?

_____

_____

What do you think it means to *labor in vain* in a marriage?

_____

_____

When we allow the Lord to build our marriage relationship from the ground up, and we choose to live within His chain of command with each spouse doing his or her part, our "house" will become beautiful inside and out, a shining testimony of God's presence in our lives.

THE BLUEPRINT

In this chapter we will discover what the Word says about marriage — including our role as wives — and discuss some practical suggestions that will do more to freshen up your house than being on *Trading Spaces!* These truths apply to all of us, whether we're single, widowed, happily married, or divorced, because God's plan for marriage is actually a beautiful love story of Christ's love for His bride, the church.

Like a classic love story, we are all the "damsels in distress," held in bondage by the cords of our sin. Christ has come as the Knight in shining armor to save us from eternal destruction and separation from Him. He willingly laid down His life for His soon-to-be bride, the church, freeing us from our captivity to sin by dying in our place. Yet not even death could overcome our almighty Savior! Triumphantly, He conquered the grave and defeated the enemy, carrying away His bride to His mansion in the sky — where they will live happily ever after. (I just love a happy ending, don't you?)

Dear friend, God adores you with all the passion a groom has for his bride. Christ didn't just die for mankind as a whole; He died for every single person He had created. He looked into the future and chose to *die for you.* If you "get" that, it will change your life! It will also transform your marriage, as you realize that you are deeply loved, whether or not you feel that love from your husband.

First John 4:19 reads, *We love because He first loved us.* That's where our love for our spouse must originate — not from the flawed human love they have for *us,* but from God's mighty *agape* love flowing within our hearts toward *them.* This amazing, self-sacrificing love is God's model for our marriages. Even though His bride was far from perfect, Christ laid down His life for her. *He chose to see beyond what she was, to what she could become with His love.* And through His strength, we're called to do the same.

Read John 15:13 and Isaiah 62:5.

According to John 15:13, is there anyone who could love you more than Jesus?

_____

How does Isaiah 62:5 describe God's feelings toward you?

_____

_____

How do these passages of Scripture encourage you?

_____

_____

What would change at your house if you adopted this sacrificial attitude toward your husband in some of the more sensitive areas of your marriage?

_____

_____

_____

Read Genesis 2:18–25.

According to verse 18, why did God design marriage in the first place?

_____

_____

_____

So what's the purpose of getting married? God said, *"It is not good for* [a] *man to be alone."* That word *good* means "pleasant, agreeable, beneficial, delightful, favorable, happy, intelligent, *best.* . . ." God wants what's *best* for us. Let's consider some principles that are found in Genesis 2:24–25 that will lay a foundation for that deep relationship we've always longed to share with our husbands.

For this reason a man will leave his father and mother and be united to his wife, and they will become one flesh. The man and his wife were both naked, and they felt no shame.

— Genesis 2:24–25

1. LEAVE.

In his Bible study, *A Biblical Portrait of Marriage,* Bruce Wilkinson explains that we are to "leave" our parents physically, financially, and emotionally when we get married, honoring them now more in the role of mentors than as our authorities.[1] "Leaving" means that our spouse is to become the second most important figure in our lives, second only to God, not Mom or Dad.[2] This is not an easy transition for parents or children, but it's vitally necessary for the next step in the process to take place.

2. CLEAVE.

For the marriage relationship to begin to take shape, children must come out from under Mom and Dad's wings and choose to cling to their spouse as their part of their covenant with God. It becomes a three-way deal! In marriage, you, your husband, and God make a promise to do it God's way: "Whereas a contract *limits* our responsibilities and *protects* our rights, in a covenant we *give up* our rights and assume our responsibilities."[3] There's a big difference! *The marriage covenant then is about laying down our lives for each other, as part of our obedience to Christ.*

3. BECOME ONE FLESH.

This is where the real fun begins! As we leave our parents and cleave to our spouses above everyone else, our "house" will become strong and durable. That wonderfully deep and intimate relationship we've always hoped for can become a reality! The Scriptures promise us that *nothing* is impossible with God, no matter what your present circumstances or past experiences. I've seen it happen over and over again — *God can work miracles in a marriage if we do things His way.*

But let's face it — this type of relationship will take work. *It's a matter of dying daily to our selfish natures and embracing "God's way" of being husband and wife.* Even if you're the only one doing it, the hardest heart can be softened if you choose to honor your husband above yourself. As hard as that is, God will bless your efforts and obedience. Galatians 6:9 promises us that in due time we will reap if we don't grow weary, so don't give up!

Read Genesis 1:27–28, 31.

What two commands did God give to the world's first newlyweds?

_____

_____

How did God feel about all He'd said and done (verse 31), and what does that tell us about God's opinion of sex within marriage?

_____

_____

The phrase "becoming one flesh" also refers to sexual intimacy. God told Adam and Eve to be _fruitful and multiply_ — _before_ sin entered the world, and He would never instruct anyone to sin. Their physical intimacy had God's blessing, and there was no reason for them to feel ashamed about it. God designed sex, within marriage, to provide pleasure and produce children, so enjoy it!

How Far We've Fallen

If these are God's true principles for marriage, then couples today are in a world of hurt. Divorce statistics demonstrate this, as they are virtually no different between believers and nonbelievers.

So often these days the corporate ladder preempts the marriage relationship, regardless of the consequences. Extramarital affairs trade the holy matrimonial relationship for casual sex and companionship, and abuse, pornography, and homosexuality continue to destroy the family, multiplying the heartache of everyone involved. The thought of marrying "'til death do us part" is now considered archaic, so when the going gets tough, either husband or wife hits the road, and the process — and the heartache — starts all over again.

So let's get real. Either marriage truly is obsolete, or Christians aren't living out their marriages according to God's design. Unfortunately, too many of us have naively fallen prey to the enemy as he launches a full-scale attack on the one institution that holds society together: the family. If he can destroy our marriages, he can cause upheaval in our families, our churches, our ministries, and even the stability of our nation. Satan's goal is to steal our faith in God and destroy our lives. Think I'm exaggerating? Let's see what the Word says about him.

Read John 10:10–11.
Contrast Jesus' goals with Satan's, as listed in this passage of Scripture.

_____

_____

_____

How can these truths relate to our marriages?

_____

_____

_____

EQUAL IN VALUE — DIFFERENT IN ROLES

And now we come to it: the infamous battle of the sexes! In corner number one we have Macho Man, full of muscle and moxie. In corner number two, it's Superwoman, 120 pounds (don't we wish) of raw self-determination and assertiveness training. If she can survive childbirth, she can do anything! Besides everyone knows, "Anything *he* can do, *she* can do better," right?

Before we even begin to approach who should do what in the marriage relationship, let me make a very important point: *Men and women are equally loved and cherished by the Creator.* We're meant to be a team, not opponents! Our role as women is every bit as important and satisfying as a man's — it's just *different!* God used women to carry out His plan throughout the Bible, from Deborah the judge, to Lydia the businesswoman, to Mary the mother of Jesus. Let's take a look at God's opinion of women as it is revealed in the Bible.

Read Genesis 17:15–16.
Do you see yourself as valuable to God, despite your weaknesses? Why or why not?

_____

_____

_____

THE PRINCESS BRIDE

God told Abraham He would give him and Sarai a son, even though Scripture later tells us *he faced the fact that his body was as good as dead* (Romans 4:19). Abraham and Sarai weren't perfect; they would later blow it with Ishmael and lie about their relationship, yet God gave them grace and blessed them with the child they had always wanted.

God could have ignored Sarai as He spoke to Abraham, and we might not have even noticed. But instead, we see the love of an adoring Father for *her,* too. I picture the conversation as something like this: God said, "Abe, let's not call her Sarai anymore. Let's call her 'princess,' because that's what she is to Me. And while I'm at it, I think I'll give her a title too. Let's call her 'The Mother of Many Nations,' because she'll play a big role in this, too, you know!"

Why did God bother to change Sarai's name? He was showing that despite her failures, He still had a great love for her — that's what that name means. And the good news is, He feels the same about each one of us! If this seems foreign to you, think about how Jesus treated the woman at the well who'd had five husbands and was living in sin, or the woman caught in adultery. He spoke to each of them with kindness and respect, in spite of their lifestyles. Jesus *elevated* the position of women, never in an inappropriate way, but as sisters in Christ.

Read Galatians 3:27–29.
According to verse 28, what promise dismisses the thought of prejudice against women in Christianity?

_____

_____

_____

_____

The book of Acts tells us that *your sons **and daughters** will prophesy* (2:17, emphasis mine). This was a huge statement in a culture where women had virtually no rights or freedom to express themselves. The gospel has liberated us to become valuable co-laborers with the King of kings! *So although men and women are certainly different in a thousand ways, we are equally valuable to God!*

The Husband's Role
as Servant Leader

Read Ephesians 5:21–33 and 1 Corinthians 11:3.

Pastor Mark Balmer explains the husband's role in this way:

> God has ordained three institutions in this world that all others are based on: the family, the government and the church. He is the head over all three, and in each of these institutions, there's not only a Godhead, but also a human head. Without a head, they can't function efficiently, and anything with two heads is a freak!
>
> . . . Marriage starts with mutual servanthood; husbands and wives submitting themselves to each other and to God. From there, when disputes arise that they just can't agree on, the husband is to act as the servant-leader of his home, not by giving commands or dominating his wife, but by loving her as Christ loved the church.[4]

The husband's role, then, is to lovingly lead and look out for the best interests of his wife (not all women), with the same fervency that Christ loves His church. That requires *his* daily submission to God, and *our* respect and willingness to let him lead. Neither can be done apart from God's strength. Yet rather than a "power trip," I think of it as God's plan for a happy, functional marriage.

Share an example of when you honored your husband by allowing him to lead, and God blessed you for it.

_____

_____

_____

_____

_____

_____

_____

The Wife's Role As Helper

Remember in Genesis 2:18 that God said He would make Adam a *helper suitable for him.* I have to admit that the whole concept of being a "helper" used to drive me crazy! Surely, I thought, I was created for more than just to clean up after my husband! Of course I was.

That word *helper* actually means "to be an ally, to further a person, to protect, restrain, and support." My role as Dave's wife isn't to be his maid (thank goodness!) and I do not wear an apron and a little hat! I'm not his dog, but I'm not his mother either! I am his equal and his friend, committed to giving him the support he needs to further him as a person. We're a team, and God's the Coach!

Since I've come to terms with that new understanding, we rarely compete anymore. I help him however I can, knowing that as I serve him, I'm serving the Lord. I have the God-given *privilege* to do all I can to bless him and create a home in which he can blossom into the man of God he was created to be. It's not a duty — it's an opportunity to strengthen the love of my life. And you know what? Both God and Dave bless me in amazing ways when I serve him in this way.

Read Proverbs 31:10–31.

Many different roles and multi-tasking abilities of women are clearly displayed in these verses. See if you can find twelve attributes of the excellent wife in this passage.

1. _____   2. _____
3. _____   4. _____
5. _____   6. _____
7. _____   8. _____
9. _____   10. _____
11. _____   12. _____

How is the woman described in this passage a team player, and what are the results of her choices? (See especially verses 28–31.)

_____

_____

_____

_____

How does this challenge you in your own marriage?

_____

_____

_____

The most important thing you can do for your marriage is to submit *yourself* to Christ's lordship, instead of praying for the Lord to change your husband first! Godly marriages form a Christ-centered triangle, where both spouses grow closer to God and to each other. But what are you to do if your husband isn't a Christian? We see from 1 Timothy 4:16 that as "you give attention to the depth of your walk, and God will take care of the breadth of it. *God* will deal with your husband as you are faithful to Him."[5]

THE SECRET OF SUBMISSION

Read 1 Peter 3:1–6.

We are instructed to come under the leadership of our husbands, even if they're disobedient to God's Word. When that's the case, what are we told to do, and not do, in verses 1 through 4 that can win them to Christ?

_____

_____

_____

_____

How can a gentle and quieted spirit speak volumes to our husbands?

_____

_____

Two principles in this passage have changed my entire understanding of how submission works. To be blunt, the Scripture tells us first to "shut up and be nice," and allow the Holy Spirit to do the talking! He's more than capable as long as we don't get in the way.

The second principle is found in verses 5 through 6: These women put their hope in God as they submitted to their husbands. Their hope wasn't being placed in their husband's ability to do the right thing. *They put their trust in God to lead, to know what was best, and to take care of them.* Sarah honored Abraham without any fear because her hope was in God, not in Abraham. Our lives are in God's hands, and He promises to work all things together for our good.

There are two exceptions to these principles. One is found in Acts 5:29 in which we are instructed to *obey God rather than men.* That's where the line is drawn in the sand. If your husband asks you to do something that blatantly goes against God's stated principles, then you are instructed to obey God rather than man. The other exception is if you are in an abusive situation — in that case, you don't have to stay, thinking that you need to be "submissive." God's plan is for husbands to lovingly lead as Christ leads the church, not for them to be domineering or abusive. If you find yourself in such a situation, get out and get help.

The key to living in submission, then, is in *our own attitude.* True submission starts in our *hearts,* and our actions follow. When we choose to allow our husbands to lead, supporting their decisions with prayer, they can blossom into the leaders they were created to be.

Read Colossians 3:17, 23–24.
How can this passage of Scripture help you keep your role as a wife in focus? How does it encourage you to obey what God commands regarding marriage?

_____

_____

_____

_____

Share about a time when you chose to honor your husband's wishes even when you didn't feel like it, and how God blessed your obedience.

_____

_____

_____

We must do *everything* as unto the Lord, confident that He will reward us either here on earth, or later in heaven. As we choose to allow our husbands to lead, praying that they will be obedient to God, we store up treasures in heaven, *regardless of the outcome here on earth.* Don't ever forget — this earth is not our home! We're just here on a temporary visa. Our true reward will be waiting for us in heaven.

Let me share with you my personal reasons of why I submit to Dave. I preface this by saying that I know I'm blessed, because I can trust that Dave will always seek to do God's will. Yet I admit I've had to learn the hard way, gritting my teeth and kicking and screaming on the inside at times! God's had His hands full teaching me this one, but I'm convinced now that it works!

FIVE REASONS I WILLINGLY SUBMIT TO DAVE

1. I do it for God because He commands it, and I've learned that as I follow His commands, our lives will truly be blessed.

2. I do it for Dave because I know it will bless every area of his life as a man and a leader.

3. I do it for our marriage because it protects it from the enemy. We have less stress, more unity and spiritual growth, a closer relationship, and a lot more fun in our home because of it!

4. I do it for our children because I want to model God's plan before them daily. I want them to see that I walk the walk, not just talk the talk, and I want these principles to be natural to them when they get married themselves someday.

5. I do it for myself because I've come to understand my *role* in God's plan has *zero* to do with my *worth* in God. I'm God's one-of-a-kind original masterpiece, just as you are! He has a special plan for me that doesn't force me to compete with Dave, and I know that God will bring it about as I'm faithful to obey Him.

Has there been an area mentioned in this chapter that is new to you, or one on which you feel compelled to work? (Notice I said *you*, not your husband!)

_____

What do you feel God is telling you to do about it?

_____

_____

_____

Make Your Marriage Come Alive

Let's say that you are a committed Christian. You and your husband have a good relationship, the house and kids are in pretty good shape, and things are on a relatively even keel at home. Yet you have this gnawing feeling that your marriage could be better. There must be something you could do to spice it up a bit!

Well, you're absolutely right! It is possible to revive your romance, jump-start your communication, break down barriers, and make your marriage fun again if you'll just take the first few steps. Let's look at four keys that can help to make a good marriage great!

1. Show the Guy Some Respect!

Respect is something that every human being desires — and deserves, to one degree or another. It's an absolute must in any marriage, no matter how hard it is to conjure up, or how long it's been since you've had it! Throughout Scripture, we find wives either "crowning" their husbands with respect, or shaming them without it.

Read Proverbs 12:4.

Think of it this way. Are you more likely to be influenced by someone who treats you kindly, or someone who treats you like you're an idiot? Which is more likely to produce a positive change in your behavior? How about when someone nags you?

Let's bring this a little closer to home. Do you ever catch yourself "preaching at" your husband, hoping you will change him? Proverbs 16:21 says that *sweetness of speech increases persuasiveness* (NASB). Being nice to your husband will go farther in persuading him to be a godly man than nagging ever will! God wants us to treat our husbands with the same respect that we desire for ourselves.

And remember that verse that talked about *do unto others*? When we honor our husbands with simple kindness, we throw the door wide open for God to work in their lives. If they don't already know God, a change in our attitude can work wonders in how they receive the gospel we live by. We must choose to be trustworthy, keeping those things confidential that we know are private to them. We *earn* their trust, and as we do, not only are they more likely to open up with us, our friendship will grow from it.

Sometimes when women complain their husbands never talk to them, it's because the guys have learned they might as well put out an APB to the entire neighborhood whenever they share a confidence with their wives. There are some women whose husbands aren't the spiritual leaders of their home, so they show their own "spirituality" by slamming them with insults, both at home and in public. This just drives their husbands farther into their shells! Good luck ever getting them to open up to their wives again, let alone be drawn to their Savior. Do you see how devastating this attitude can be? I know that it can be hard at times, but God will *honor* the wife who treats her husband with respect.

Can you see yourself in any of these scenarios? If so, which, and why?

_____

_____

_____

List some ways in which you show respect to your husband that has been helpful in your relationship.

_____

_____

_____

2. GIVE YOUR LOVE LIFE A BOOST WITH LOVE, SEX, AND ROMANCE.

We can show our husbands our love by encouraging them and building them up, being sensitive to their needs, and holding them up in prayer. Simple courtesies like making dinner, keeping the household running and yourself looking nice, and a positive attitude also go a long way toward making our husbands know they're loved and appreciated. Before you object, yes, I do still live in the real world, and with three kids I know how some days it takes all your strength just to survive! But kindness is definitely something we should shoot for!

This sort of kindness can go a long way toward rekindling the love and romance that may have gone AWOL in your marriage. You'll be surprised how *acting* lovingly toward your husband will increase your loving feelings, and can heighten the intimacy and romance that you may feel that you have lost.

Read 1 Corinthians 7:3–5.

In his book *His Needs, Her Needs*, author Willard F. Harley, Jr. says that sexual intimacy tops the list of the top five needs of men, even though it doesn't even appear on the women's list![6] But as we make the effort to meet our husband's sexual needs, we show him how special he is to us. If your love life has become routine, or isn't enjoyable to you, talk to him about it. Chances are he doesn't know what's important to you, and he won't unless you tell him. Then take the initiative to plan a romantic evening that will stretch into a special night. If you'll take the lead in this area, he'll love you for it, and it will be a lot more fun for you, too!

3. SPEAK THE TRUTH IN LOVE.

Read Ephesians 4:15.

How could this verse be applied to the marriage relationship?

_____

_____

_____

How might following this principle improve your own marriage?

_____

_____

_____

"I will speak the truth in love, and willingly receive it from you." Those words were part of Dave's and my wedding vows. Little did I know how hard they would be to live out! When Dave brings up an area of my life that needs some attention, I usually don't want to hear it! It may be a blind spot, or it may be something I know about but don't feel like dealing with at that time. But when I pray about it and discover that he's right, God enables me to work toward change in that area. If after praying about it, I still don't see it his way, I just give the situation to God and ask Him to reveal His will to me.

I gently do the same when I see something in Dave's life that needs to be addressed. God tends to work on our rough edges through the relationships He places in our lives, and our spouse is often His sharpest tool! These relationships help us both grow . . . and stay humble!

On the other hand, there's also a time to be quiet! Let's face it: Women love to talk. It's said that the average woman speaks over 25,000 words a day, while men tend to speak only 15,000. It's no wonder that our guys run out of things to say long before we do!

When we commune with God, He offers us grace, mercy, and a listening ear every single time we come to Him. He doesn't interrupt, or start out by telling us what we've done wrong. He listens. He cares, and with arms of compassion He holds us until we're ready to face the world again. Likewise, when talking with our husbands, sometimes a period of silence while they unwind is the best gift we can give to them!

4. BE LOYAL.
Read 1 Corinthians 6:9–11 and Matthew 5:27–28.

The Bible is very clear about God's standards concerning sex outside of marriage. It's wrong. Whether you're married and are sexually active with someone other than your husband (adultery), or single and having sex apart from marriage (fornication), the consequences are clear. Save yourself some misery. Don't go there.

If you're in a sexually active relationship outside of marriage, I encourage you to break it off and make yourself accountable to someone. We know of several couples who have temporarily separated, later resumed their relationship God's way, and are now happily married! Of course it's not easy, but it can be done.

Thankfully, most of us are not in that situation, but the passage we just read in the book of Matthew tells us about another sin of disloyalty that can catch us off guard if we're not careful. Developing emotional ties with someone of the opposite sex is equally devastating and just as potentially dangerous to a marriage. This occurs when we find ourselves sharing more freely with a friend or co-worker than we do with our spouse. One opens up, the other listens, and before they know it, an emotional bond has formed — a bond that's free from the responsibilities and reality of life. If that's you, be warned: You're paving the way for an extramarital affair.

The Bible instructs us to *abstain from all appearance of evil* (1 Thessalonians 5:22 KJV). As harmless as these attachments may seem at first, God looks at our hearts, and He knows when we secretly desire more of a relationship with someone than we should. It's been said that sin will take you farther than you want to go, keep you there longer than you want to stay, and cost you more than you want to pay. We put our marriages and our families, as well as our financial and spiritual well-being, on the line when we don't guard our hearts in this way.

THERE'S HOPE IF YOU'RE DIVORCED OR SEEKING A MATE

Many marriages don't make it. Whether because of infidelity or a host of other reasons, some relationships die . . . and part of each spouse dies with them. Yet it's crucial to know that *although God hates the pain and suffering divorce causes, He still loves the people involved.*

Do you remember the woman at the well, divorced five times and living with another man? There was no condemnation in Jesus' voice when He addressed her sins. Instead, we find the same amazing compassion He extends to each one of us, no matter what we've done. God *chooses* to remove our sins from us as far as the east is from the west, and He is the healer of broken hearts. As you allow God to help you forgive and work through the hurt and the pain, He can restore your life. He will meet you where you are, with open arms and a heart full of mercy.

If you're single and desiring to be married, pray, get plugged into a small group of Christian fellowship, and keep actively serving at church. Then be patient! Let the words of Proverbs 3:5–6 encourage you: *Trust in the LORD with all your heart and lean not on your own understanding; in all your ways acknowledge him, and he will make your paths straight.* That's His promise to you! Trust Him — don't try to figure it all out on your own. Acknowledge His ability to work things out for you, and *He will do it!*

 I kept a little card in my Bible while I was waiting for God to bring a godly man into my life. It said, "God gives the best to those who leave the choice to Him." God is faithful, and if you can trust Him for your salvation, you can surely trust Him to give you a husband! I did, and it worked. Remember this: *His timing + your obedience = His plan!*

Regardless of your marital situation, there's still only one way to true, lifelong fulfillment deeper than even the best marriage could ever give. Draw close to God, trust His leading, obey His Word, and you will experience the incredible love of an adoring Father that no relationship on earth could ever duplicate.

PRAYER

Lord, You know all about me. You understand every detail of my marital situation. Help me be the wife you want me to be. Give me the love, patience, and perseverance I need to be a godly helper for my husband. Direct my words and my steps to build this marriage up rather than tear it down. Forgive my shortcomings and renew my hope, Lord. Help me to see my husband, or even my ex-husband, through Your eyes. I commit myself anew to Your lordship in this area. In Jesus' name. Amen.

SUMMARY POINTS

- Unless the Lord builds the house, we labor in vain.
- God calls husbands and wives to leave, cleave, and become one flesh.
- Although men and women's roles are different, their value to God is equal.
- The secret of submission is to put our trust in *God,* more than in our mates.

FROM PRINT TO POWER: PERSONAL APPLICATION

1. A wise person once said, "The secret to a good marriage is not so much finding the right person as being the right person." With that in mind, write down any ideas you might have concerning "being the right person" that could make your marriage better.

2. Next, ask your husband if you could discuss one thing each of you would like each other to do or change in your relationship. Take a minute to jot down any ideas, including possible ideas to add some fun to your marriage, and then set a time to discuss it. Don't expect immediate results, but over time this should make a positive difference in your marriage.

One example I made up is planning a "Husband Appreciation Day." It turns an ordinary day into a celebration, starting with his favorite meal, and then something special that he enjoys doing. We sometimes go out for dinner and a movie, go on a family bike ride, take a walk in the park, get tickets to a game, go out for ice cream, or whatever else he wants to do. When the kids were little, they'd have fun being included in this by contributing "secret messages" on napkins at dinner, or wrapping up homemade gifts for Daddy. It's a great way to teach your kids about giving to others — and make your husband feel loved and appreciated at the same time.

3. If you've been through a divorce, ask God to show you any unforgiveness that might be still tucked away in your heart. Record what He shows you, and then take these thoughts and attitudes to Him in prayer. You might ask a strong Christian friend to join you for prayer support.

4. If you're single and desiring to get married, make a list of the godly characteristics that are important to you in a mate, and keep it in your Bible where you can pray about it often. God knows you better than anyone else does, and as you "delight yourself in Him" He will give you the desires of your heart (see Psalm 37:4).

CHAPTER 9

OUR CHILDREN — OUR TREASURES

"Sons are a heritage from the LORD, children a reward from him."

— Psalm 127:3

It wasn't that long ago that the thought of motherhood totally overwhelmed me. Before I knew God, my plan was to become a hardcore investigative reporter, and I thought that having kids would just get in the way. My whole life was focused on my plans, my dreams, and doing things *my* way. Fortunately, God changed my heart and gave my husband and me three of the best children anyone could ever ask for. And with them came a radical change of life!

Knee-deep in diapers and toys, there were days I felt sure I'd taken a wrong turn somewhere. I was torn between what *I* wanted and what *they* needed, and although I adored them dearly, learning to be a full-time mom didn't come easily for me. Dave was traveling extensively at that time, and many days and nights I cried out to the Lord to help me just to survive!

I wanted so badly to be out *doing something tangible* — accomplishing anything that felt more substantial than just raising children. I couldn't see that nurturing and training them on a daily basis was accomplishing a great deal — in God's eternal scheme of things. Instead, many days it felt more like I needed to wear a black-and-white striped shirt and a whistle around my neck!

Eighteen years later we find that Kristi, Luke, and Anna are truly treasures from heaven and bring so much joy into our lives. Being parents has been the hardest, and yet the most rewarding, job we've ever attempted. In fact, as the day approaches for Kristi to leave for college, and someday possibly the mission field, my heart is torn again between great joy and great longing for days gone by. Do you think she'd mind if I went with her to hold her hand as she faces new challenges, or to wipe away her tears on the hard days? Yeah, right! God gives us an amazing love for our children that's deeper than we could ever imagine, but it is a mirror of His love toward *us*.

If you're a mother, do you think of your children as treasures, tagalongs, or tyrants? In the lines below, share what motherhood has taught you.

_____

_____

_____

_____

Children have a way of keeping us humble and seeking God for wisdom. If there's anything I've learned, it's that raising children to become godly adults will happen *only* as we lean — and lean hard — on our own heavenly Father.

As we tackle this huge topic of raising children, it might help us to work backward. Let's begin by considering what we want our children to take with them when they leave home. How are we preparing them to be godly adults? Will they have learned, or "caught," enough from us to continue to pursue God's best in their lives when they're out on their own? Will they have a passion for God, a healthy fear of Him that will guide and protect them throughout their lives? It's as if God deposits His beautiful babies on the doorsteps of our lives, with little notes attached that read, "Teach them how to live for Me."

The bottom line is that our children belong to God, and they have been made in His image to fulfill His purposes. We are merely the stewards of their souls. *Think of that! The almighty God trusts His most valuable creations to us to raise them up for Him. Doesn't He know how badly we mess up on a daily basis? Of course He does, but even so, parenthood is part of His plan, so we'd better dig out those instructions!*

INVEST IN GOD'S PURPOSES

In his book, *Shepherding a Child's Heart,* author Ted Tripp explains, "[Children] need to understand that all of life rushes toward the day when we shall stand before God and give an account."[1] God gives them to us for a "spring training" season of sorts, to prepare them for whatever "big game" God has ahead for them. Like a good coach — or a bad one — we will make a lasting imprint in their young lives, for better or worse!

Our job is to prepare our children for all that life will bring their way; to function independently under God's authority; to be responsible, hard workers, able to handle both success and failure; to serve others, to master a myriad of practical skills; and ultimately, to answer to God. Talk about a tall order! It is too tall, in fact, to be accomplished through our limited wisdom. *This kind of task calls for my most eloquent prayer: "HEEEELLPP!!!"*

Read Matthew 25:14–30.

What is the underlying principle of this parable?

_____

_____

How can it apply to parenting?

_____

_____

As moms, what are some ways in which we can we be like the faithful servant in this parable?

_____

_____

The "treasures" God has given us are eating at our dinner tables and sleeping in our beds! We can think of the eighteen-plus years while our children live with us as our capital investment in their lives. *God gives us the choice either to make a permanent investment in who they will become while their hearts are soft and moldable — or to be lazy, too busy to care, or too worried we don't know enough to teach them anything spiritual.*

If we don't make this deposit in their hearts while we have the opportunity, when they need to make a withdrawal later in life, their accounts will be empty! But if we're faithful with the much or the little that God has given us, He will give us the wisdom, grace, and patience we need to raise our children up in godliness. *We can choose to invest our lives into something that will outlast us; that is, the souls of men and women, and pave the way for a legacy of sold-out Christianity for generations to come.* What an incredible opportunity! Show me a corporate job that offers higher rewards than that!

Let's take a look at how we use our time, and let's be real. Does anything matter to you more than your family? How about your career? Your personal goals? Your church or community involvement? A clean house?! These are all part of that never-ending juggling act we moms attempt on a daily basis. We manage to keep ninety-nine balls in the air, but there is always that one pesky ball on the floor! Let's see which "balls" God's Word says are vitally important — and which ones we can allow ourselves to drop!

TEN TRUTHS OUR CHILDREN NEED TO KNOW

In addition to the Ten Commandments, of course, there are certain truths from Scripture that your children need to know. Read the following passages and for each, list one truth that your children need to learn from you.

SCRIPTURE	TRUTH
1. John 3:16–17	_____
2. Proverbs 4:23	_____
3. John 14:6	_____
4. 1 John 2:3–6	_____
5. Proverbs 9:10	_____
6. Ephesians 2:10	_____
7. Matthew 16:24–27	_____
8. Ephesians 6:1–3	_____
9. Psalm 119:9, 11	_____
10. Colossians 3:23–24	_____

Which of these verses challenge you in how you are parenting your children? How does it do so? What will you do about this challenge?

_____

_____

_____

_____

How Am I Supposed to Do All That?

I know exactly what many of you are thinking: *This woman must have a lot more time than I do!* Probably not. Putting these lessons to work in your life won't happen in a day, but the Word does show us how to incorporate them into our busy schedules and work toward these goals.

Read Deuteronomy 6:4–9.

In what ways does this passage tell us to teach our kids about God?

_____

_____

What are some practical ideas to do this that have worked at your house?

_____

_____

_____

Training Their Hearts

Ted Tripp explains his concept of the training he calls "shepherding their hearts" like this:

> The parenting task is multi-faceted. It involves being authorities who are kind, shepherding your children to understand themselves in God's world, and keeping the gospel in clear view so your children can internalize the good news and someday live in mutuality with you as people under God…. The purpose for your authority in the lives of your children is not to hold them under your power, but to empower them to be self-controlled people living freely under the authority of God.[2]

The time, prayer, discipline, and love we invest in their training can make all the difference in who they become. It's the best gift we can ever give them. Dave and I have found that as our children learn that they're accountable to God, our job becomes a lot easier! They not only answer to us when they disobey, they answer to God, and understanding that truth helps them keep in line when we're not around.

Read Ephesians 6:1–3 and Proverbs 22:6.

What commandment is given specifically to children, and what promises accompany it?

_____

_____

What promise do parents have as they make an effort to train (which means "to instruct and discipline") their children on a consistent basis?

_____

_____

_____

If our children have been taught God's Word, and have seen it modeled before them through our integrity, they will always have that reference point to look back upon, even if they're not serving the Lord. It worked for the prodigal son — so don't give up if it has yet to happen in your child's life. Keep praying; our God is able.

TOUGH LOVE IS TRUE LOVE

I was in traffic recently behind a young driver who made me nervous. She was chomping at the bit to make a left turn into heavy traffic, and I found myself praying for her safety at every intersection. She didn't seem ready to be driving alone, and it looked as if she needed protection from herself! *No matter how unpopular it makes us, we owe it to our kids to say no when it is necessary, for their safety if for no other reason.*

As we teach our children to live under the safety umbrella of God's Word, and demonstrate to them the importance of honoring His authority and ours, we can spare them years of hardship. *Appropriate, loving discipline should focus on restoring their relationship with us and with God, without condemnation.* It's important to note that when the Scriptures talk about using "the rod," it refers to various levels of appropriate correction — not just spanking. *Biblical discipline is controlled,* as opposed to hitting or slapping in anger, which is abusive.

Read Proverbs 13:24; 29:15, 17 and Hebrews 12:11.

According to these passages, how are our children helped by discipline? How are they hurt without it?

_____

_____

_____

Spring Training Manual

Here are some tips for the "spring training" of your kid's lives!

• Pray for each of your children every single day, early in the day, for wisdom, health, and protection, and that they'll serve God with their whole hearts.

• Give each of them your love and encouragement every single day, and never stop giving them hugs. Let them know that you believe in them, that they are God's special creation, and that He has big plans for their lives.

• Deposit God's Word in them through sharing Bible stories and family devotions. Filling their hearts with God's Word will be their best protection throughout life.

• Set firm, reasonable boundaries, and then stick with them!

• Teach them that even when we as parents are wrong, we need to repent to receive God's forgiveness, and apologize to whomever we've offended. As we model how we expect them to act, they will learn humility, will be taught to ask forgiveness, and will be pointed to the Savior by our example.

• Listen and communicate! Share what God is teaching you at this time in your life. Aim to have a meaningful conversation with each of your children daily, even if it's only a brief one. If you think something is bothering them, ask them about it, and then really _listen,_ even when it's not convenient.

• Take inventory of your children's lives regularly. Evaluate how they are doing spiritually, socially, emotionally, and academically, and make adjustments accordingly.

• Help your children develop their gifts for God's glory, and teach them practical things like good manners, as well as how to cook, clean, manage their money wisely, and other daily living skills.

• Teach them that tomorrow we answer to God and are rewarded for how we spent our lives today. Teach your children that their self-worth comes from Him, and rather than just fostering a good "self-esteem" within themselves, they should also esteem God for all He's done for us![3]

• Take time to play with your kids, saving some of your "down time" and energy for them. Plan activities, special days, or vacations that will build memories as a family. Capture little bits of time to show them your love and attention.

• Model what you believe every day, knowing that your actions will always speak louder than words. Let your kids see you praying, reading the Bible, and serving God, and show them how He picks you up when you fall. Be sure to celebrate with your kids when God answers prayers!

Read 1 Timothy 4:16.

What does God ask us to do in this verse, and what is His promise that accompanies these actions?

_____

_____

How does this promise apply to how we parent our children?

_____

_____

_____

Making Devotions Actually Work

Probably the most important thing that my husband and I have ever done with our kids is to have family devotions. We started this practice years ago when they were young, and after a great deal of trial and error, we've come up with a system that actually works!

We read through ten to fifteen verses of a book of the Bible, one at a time, a couple of nights a week, stopping after each one to discuss how each one applies to our daily lives. The kids ask questions, and then we each pray out loud for each other's needs and the various needs of our friends, our relatives, and missionaries from our church.

This devotional practice has literally changed our lives. I can even honestly say that most nights the kids actually enjoy it! It's their chance to be heard by their family and to get answers for what is going on in their lives. And although Satan usually fights it every step of the way, our devotions have become for us a rich time of learning and drawing close as a family.

Here are some keys that have made this work in our family, and could be helpful in yours:

1. First, pray that everyone in your family would get along during devotions! Pray strongly against any distractions that would come to impede this special time, deciding beforehand to ignore them if they do come, *including* the phone.

2. Keep your devotional time short (no more than thirty minutes).

3. Let each person bring a snack to the table to keep their mouths and hands busy. (This may be the most important suggestion when your children are younger!)

4. Don't put your devotions off until everyone is home. When it's time, go ahead and begin.

5. Don't feel guilty if you miss a week. Just keep trying!

Read 2 Timothy 3:14–17.
According to this passage, what are some of the ways in which our children will benefit if we take the time to teach them God's Word?

_____

_____

_____

_____

_____

_____

HINDRANCES TO THESE GOALS

Some of you may be thinking, *Didn't you say at the beginning of this study that some of the balls I'm juggling I should drop? But all I'm getting is more and more tasks to add to my "to do" list!*

I totally understand how frustrating our busy schedules can be. All of these things — spending quality time with our kids, family devotions, training our children in the Word of God — take time and energy, two of the scarcest resources for most of us! But does that mean we should just give up? No way! Instead, let's examine some things that we may be doing that *don't* work toward these goals, and see if there are any things that we can subtract.

1. PUTTING ANYTHING AHEAD OF OUR RELATIONSHIP WITH GOD.

Read Matthew 10:37.

When we put anything — including our kids or our husbands — above God, everything in our lives gets out of whack. God must be over all; and after that our first priorities should be our marriage, and then our children. Obviously this is not easy to do — usually our kids make their needs known the loudest. And anybody who has ever had a husband with the flu knows that they can make their needs known pretty loudly too!

Our relationship with God must come first, no matter what is going on with our children or our husband, but use common sense. If your child is sick, don't head off to church anyway and neglect your child. That's not godly; that's neglect. Yet we must guard ourselves against always putting our kids at the top of the heap in our households. *They shouldn't be calling the shots; God should be, and we should all be following Him together.*

Another dangerous practice is that of putting your kids first before your marriage. When Mom or Dad's attention consistently goes to the kids first, with no thought of each other, things are out of order. Eventually the children will move out, and then what will be left? Our marriage vows said, "Until death do us part," not "Until *kids* do us part!"

God's way puts our spouses first — then our children, and in that arrangement, everybody's needs will be met. Never forget that a broken marriage will cost kids more than it does for their mom to invest a few hours into a healthy one.

When we neglect God's priorities in the family, it can lead to all kinds of trouble. If a husband feels short-changed by his wife, he may make up for her lack of attention by choosing to spend more time at the office, more time playing sports, more time with his buddies, spend more money, or even be pulled into an extra-marital affair as he grows more and more distant from home and family.

The same danger exists for women, especially if her husband is becoming less involved at home. She may choose to spend more money or more hours at the office, more time with friends, eat more food, or even fall into an affair as she searches for the love she should be receiving from her mate. God's plan for all parents is that both husband and wife love Him first, cherish each other, and raise their children as a team.

Have you ever seen a family get thrown out of balance when the kids were allowed to be in charge? What was the result?

_____

_____

_____

2. GIVING OUR KIDS MATERIAL POSSESSIONS INSTEAD OF OURSELVES.
Read Proverbs 23:4–5.

True joy is not found in the abundance of things. If we could only grasp this concept, it would totally change the focus of most of our parenting. When we become busy with our own lives, it's easy to fall into the trap of giving our kids *things* to make up for our lack of *time* with them. This is especially hard when there's been a divorce, and a parent only gets to "spoil" their kids on a limited basis. We all love our children, and most of us want to show them our love every way possible.

Yet I have found that most of the time, my kids really want *me* more than the stuff I can give them. Those extra hours spent at the office to be able to buy your children "all of the good things in life" says more about what *you* want than what *they* really want. Most kids would really rather have their parents home more of the time than they want the never-ending lists of things they say they need.

Ted Tripp puts it like this:

> We teach them to find their soul's delight in going places and doing things. We attempt to satisfy their lust for excitement. We fill their young lives with distractions from God. We give them material things and take delight in their delight in possessions. Then we hope that somewhere down the line they will see that a life worth living is found only in knowing and serving God.[4]

When we know the joy of knowing and serving God ourselves, we understand that nothing else can come close. Let's pass that truth on to our children! Of course, we can still bless our kids with the things they need and want, but we do them a disservice when we make "things" the center of their world. Instead, let's steer them away from a lifestyle of pursuing wealth for wealth's sake, and *toward* a life of fulfillment in doing God's will.

Worldly wealth is temporary, but the rewards of living for God are eternal. Pursuing wealth always leaves us craving more, but living for God leaves us satisfied and full of joy! Which do you want for your kids?

How do you make time to have fun with your kids? What means the most to them? A special date, a favorite vacation, or cuddling up together on the weekends with a good book?

_____

_____

_____

_____

3. Going in Too Many Directions at Once.
Read Proverbs 31:27–29.
Who appreciates the sacrifices of the Proverbs 31 woman as she keeps the affairs of her household intact?

_____

Who else might appreciate her efforts, even though they are not specifically mentioned in these verses?

_____

_____

We pay a high price when we allow ourselves or our families to become overcommitted. Nothing has broken my heart as a mother like knowing that my schedule had caused me to disappoint my child. A missed ballgame, an overlooked performance, or even the ten minutes it takes to read a story — there's just never enough time to go around!

The same is true when we allow our children to be involved in too many activities. Family unity goes down the drain when everyone is always running in opposite directions. When we allow our kids to agree to participate in every single opportunity that comes along, they never have any "down time." We all know those kids who are routinely picked up early from one practice only to arrive late to another! That's no way to be a kid!

In our family, my husband and I have set limits on what each child can be involved in at one time. Some kids can handle more than others and still function happily, but when their schedules eliminate any family time, it has become too much. "Down time" is where creativity begins and relationships are built. Your kids still have plenty of years ahead of them to live under the tyranny of crazy schedules that most adults do!

But there is hope for even the craziest adult schedule! This "tyranny" under which we live can still be tamed. I've got a three-step plan for those days when there's no way everything can get done! I should know — I have lots of them!

• Relax — Take a deep breath!
• Remember your priorities, and
• Refocus — Forget the chaos and zero in on what's absolutely essential today.

If you're employed, think about your job for a minute. Does it allow you to be the mom you want to be, or are there changes that could make it work better for your family? Have you prayed and asked God whether or not He wants you working in the first place? Some jobs work well with a family, and some don't.

Think also about your church and community commitments. Some of you who are reading this would benefit from becoming more involved, but there are others of you who need to let some things go for the sake of your marriages and families.

What is God speaking to your heart about your schedule and your priorities?

_____

_____

Do your hours away from home allow you to meet your family's needs, or are changes necessary?

_____

_____

What things do you feel God is telling you to add to your schedule?

_____

_____

What things might He be telling you to drop?

_____

_____

Over the years I have learned the importance of praying before saying "yes" to any commitment I make, trying to be careful to save time to meet my husband and family's needs first. This is a discipline that has been very hard for me to learn, yet I know I won't regret it, no matter what it requires me to lay aside, because remember, I get one shot to influence them for God's glory!

4. HAVING LOOSE BOUNDARIES OR LOW STANDARDS.

Read Proverbs 6:20–23.

Give an example of a high standard or firm boundary your own parents or another mentor in your life set for you that became a positive shaping influence in your life.

_____

_____

_____

_____

I used to think if I had an expectation that my children didn't meet, I was expecting too much. Sometimes the goals that parents set aren't age-appropriate, and a compromise is best. But often, lowering an expectation actually robs children of the chance to work harder to achieve it! For both adults and children, struggles produce character as we stretch to reach the goals that are set before us.

Firm, loving boundaries will give our children security and keep everyone on track. Our kids need us to be their *parents* first, and their *friends* second, just as Christ is our Lord first and after that our Friend. There will always be days in which the decisions you make as a parent won't make you popular, as you prayerfully direct your kids toward making godly choices. Yet you do your children a great disservice when your *primary* goal is to be their friend. Be their parent, and when they're old enough to understand, they'll be glad that you were.

God's standard is perfection, which we can never achieve (see Matthew 5:48). That's why we need a Savior in the first place! Knowing God's standard keeps us humble before God and brings us back to the Cross where we receive His mercy and grace.

5. Overlooking the Motives of Our Children's Hearts.

Read 1 Samuel 16:7.

Using this verse as a guide, what lesson should we teach our children when they do the right thing, but we know their motive is wrong?

_____

_____

_____

_____

God is more concerned with the motive of our hearts than He is with our actions. When we correct our child's behavior without addressing the motive behind that behavior, we are in danger of producing self-righteous little brats! They may begin to think like this about their schoolmates or friends: *I follow more rules than you do, so I'm better than you.* But we know that's not true! Our best works are as filthy rags unless we have been washed in the blood of the Lamb.

Think of the wise young ruler who told Jesus he'd kept the law from his youth throughout his lifetime. He was self-righteous, and Jesus challenged the greed in his heart by saying, "Go, sell all you have . . . " (see Matthew 19:16–26). Outwardly the young man looked good, but on the inside, his motives were terribly impure, and he needed to be forgiven. Along the same line, what about the Pharisee who proudly bragged about his righteous lifestyle, and compared himself to the tax gatherer who simply begged for mercy? Jesus said that it was the *sinner* who had found mercy because of his humble heart (see Luke 18:9–14).

There are several ways that you can address heart issues with your children. One way is to help them recognize the motives behind their actions. After Joey takes a toy from his brother, we can help him see that he took the toy because of selfishness, but that God will forgive him and can help him be more loving in the future. We can also come alongside our children and explain that even we as parents need Jesus to forgive our mistakes and help us too. Handling heart issues like this will help our kids get into the habit of coming to Christ for help and forgiveness, rather than "faking" their way through "counterfeit Christianity."

THE DESTRUCTIVENESS OF FAVORITISM

Read Genesis 37:3–4.

How can showing favoritism to one child over another be so detrimental to their lives?

_____

_____

_____

Let's face it: Some kids are easier to love than others! Their obedient hearts and their sweet spirits make them a joy to be around. Others take more work to understand them and then channel them toward God's direction for their lives. But when we favor one child over another with our time, money, or attention, we set all of them up for problems, both now and in the future.

Favoritism caused absolute hatred between Joseph and his brothers. *Ironically, their father, who only wanted to bless his child, actually hurt him by playing favorites.* I'm sure that Jacob never dreamed that the blessings he showered on Joseph would land his favorite son in a pit waiting to be sold into slavery!

Each one of us — including each one of our children — is a treasure to God, and His grace is sufficient to handle even the most challenging child. He proves that by choosing to love *us!*

Hope for Single Parents

Sadly, there are a huge percentage of single parents today, doing their best to raise their children in a godly manner and be both mother and father to them. For those of you in this position, my hat is off to you. There are days when I wonder if I will survive raising three kids *with* a Christian husband by my side, let along trying it as a single mom.

God promises, *My grace is sufficient for you, for power is perfected in weakness* (2 Corinthians 12:9 NASB), He will *not fail you or forsake you* (Deuteronomy 31:6 NASB), He will be your husband (see Isaiah 54:5), and His mercies are *new every morning* (Lamentations 3:23). Friend, God hasn't forgotten you, and *absolutely nothing* can separate you from His love.

The Cost of Biblical Parenting

I wish I could say that raising children to become responsible, God-fearing adults is easy. It may be the hardest thing we'll ever do — yet nothing will ever be more important. It will require more energy than we have, more time than we feel like giving, more money than we ever dreamed, more sacrifice than we feel we can bear, and a whole lot more patience than Job!

All of this may not sound very encouraging, but it is, because we were never meant to do it apart from God's strength. If we're leaning hard on God because we know we can't do it ourselves, that's exactly where we're supposed to be! The book of James says that the struggles we face will produce godly character in us (see 1:2–4). That's why we can *consider it joy* when we go through these trials, because God uses the trials with our kids to mold *us* as much as we're trying to mold *them!*

When our kids finally move out on their own, I pray that they'll take these three life lessons with them: (1) No matter what, they can always come to us for help; (2) Without

God, they can do nothing; and (3) Through Him, they can do all things. Proverbs 31:31 promises that when we live for God, love our husbands, and raise our children in the ways of the Lord, we will be rewarded. So let's go for it!

PRAYER

Father, You know my heart. I try so hard to be a good parent, and yet I miss the mark so often. Please empower me to be a loving mother, steering my children toward all that is godly and away from all that can harm them. I rely on Your power, Lord, and I dedicate myself anew to doing it Your way. In Jesus' name I pray. Amen.

SUMMARY POINTS

• God has entrusted our children to us as the stewards of their souls.

• Training our children's hearts in righteousness takes prayer, patience, discipline, and lots of love.

• Putting our children ahead of our relationship with God or with our husbands can be detrimental to both our children and our marriages.

• Biblical parenting is costly, but it is worth it eternally.

FROM PRINT TO POWER: PERSONAL APPLICATION

1. Do you feel that you honor your relationship with God above your relationship with your husband or children? Do you manage to set aside time with God on a regular basis? If you're married, do you save time to nurture your relationship with your husband and keep it fresh? Pray about any challenges you might have in these areas, and record any ways in which you feel God might be asking you to make a change.

2. Do your children know that they're more important to you than your job or ministry commitments? Do you model how to serve others in front of them, without neglecting their own needs? If not, in what ways might you need to change?

_____

_____

_____

_____

3. Look over the lists given on pages 163 and 164, and then pick several of the topics that touch your heart. Pray about them, and then list any changes God might be asking you to make.

_____

_____

_____

_____

4. Which "Hindrances to These Goals" (see pages 166–172) are a part of your normal routine? Pray about each of these, and again, list any changes or adjustments you feel God might be asking you to make.

_____

_____

_____

_____

5. Look back over the goals you set for your children in chapter four (see page 81). What do you want them to know spiritually, physically, academically, relationally, and financially before they grow older and eventually leave home? At this stage in their lives, are your children "on track" for learning these lessons? What changes might you need to make in your parenting strategies for these goals to be met?

_____

_____

_____

_____

_____

_____

_____

_____

_____

_____

CHAPTER 10

WALKING IN FREEDOM AND VICTORY

"I can do all things through Christ who strengthens me."
— Philippians 4:13 NKJV

Long ago I knew a young girl who was raised in a loving Christian home, but she insisted on leaving the truths she had learned there and finding her own way. She made a brief commitment to Christ in high school, but soon fell away. Before long she was deeply involved in an unhealthy relationship, and she began drinking alcohol on a regular basis. Thinking God could never forgive her for the things in which she had become involved, she gave up trying to live for Him and spiraled down deeper and deeper into the ways of the world, searching for the love and acceptance that only He could give.

Before long, alcohol had its grip on her life, and she soon crossed the line into despair. As she stumbled from one party to the next, pulling many friends down with her, her heavenly Father continued to woo her to come back to Him. Once she tried to take baby steps toward Him, but then she fell hard again, and found herself with no reason to live. In utter despair, she threw herself on the grace of God, unsure if even He could help her in the state she was in.

As the years began to pass, although her steps were slippery, God was faithful to pick her up and give her the grace she needed to keep growing closer to Him. Unfortunately, in her efforts to change, she mistakenly exchanged her yoke of sin for a yoke of slavery to condemnation for past mistakes, until she learned that that, too, had to go. Eventually she came to understand that God had allowed the hard times in her life to take place so that her roots would go deep in Him.

As she spent more and more time in His Word, her priorities, goals, habits, friends, and even her quiet time with Him changed and blossomed, and a new sense of purpose came into her life. Eventually God brought a godly man into her life, and they married, had children, and even went into the ministry together. *She had truly been redeemed by the grace of God.* Finally, God led her to write a study that could help others find the same amazing grace that she had experienced, the study you're holding in your hands right now . . .

I'm no stranger to obstacles. I can truly empathize with you as you face challenges in your life, and I can relate as I continue to deal with the struggles that come my way. And yet, I can say to you with all the passion in my soul, *you can do whatever God calls you to do, through His power and grace.* He will do His work through you, as you cooperate with the Holy Spirit and abide in the Vine. As you obey God and live within His boundaries, His grace and power will abound for you.

In their book, *Experiencing God,* authors Henry Blackaby and Claude V. King write:

> When you believe that nothing significant can happen through you, you have said more about your belief in *God* than you have said about *yourself....* The truth is He is able to do anything He pleases with one ordinary person fully consecrated to Him.[1]

Are you willing to face the things that hold you back? If so, God will meet you where you are, take you by the hand, and walk with you through the fire. As you begin to read this chapter, I challenge you to trust Him with the hard things in your life. *Choose to believe that He loves you enough to do what's best for you.*

What are some things that have been holding you back from living the life God wants for you?

_____

_____

_____

_____

As we tackle the obstacles in our lives, nothing will help us as much as the Word of God, so this chapter is loaded with scripture passages. So grab your Bible and let's get started!

TRIALS THAT TRANSFORM

Have you ever wondered why God allows us to suffer if He loves us so much? Is there a purpose in our trials, or has He just gone to sleep on the job?

The first thing we must understand is that God uses trials for our benefit. They *can* transform us, if we learn to walk through them God's way. God is still in control and knows what He's doing, even when we don't have a clue what's going on! We simply obey, and trust Him with our circumstances.

Read Romans 8:28.

What promise regarding our struggles is given in this verse?

_____

_____

How could this promise affect your outlook on life?

_____

_____

_____

The promise found in Romans 8:28 doesn't mean that every situation in which we find ourselves is actually *good*. We live in a fallen world where God has given fallen man the freedom of choice, and the destruction, pain, and struggles of mankind are the result of those sinful choices. Consider, for example, the Holocaust, September 11th, or the tragedies that play themselves out every night on the evening news. These are not good in and of themselves, but God can bring good fruit from horrific hardships. He brings beauty from ashes: Corrie Ten Boom survived the Holocaust, and then brought the gospel to untold thousands as she shared how her faith had carried her through unbelievable suffering.

Americans sat in disbelief on September 11, 2001, as we watched the security we'd taken for granted for so long go up in smoke. As heartbreaking stories dominated our airwaves in the aftermath, we struggled to come to terms with the tremendous loss of life and seemingly senseless suffering that had taken place within our own borders. Yet as the debris was cleared and the details pieced together, beautiful stories of courage and faith began to emerge: an entire office staff coming to the Lord before they slipped into eternity; churches overflowing with people hungry for answers; multitudes renewing their faith and trust in God as the war on terror began. These are the fruits — the good things — that our almighty God brought from that place of suffering. *In His wisdom and mercy, God sometimes allows people to suffer temporarily to draw them closer to Him, rather than to suffer for all eternity without Him.*

Please understand — I'm not saying that your sorrow is good, or even that it was God's plan. I would never diminish the pain that so many have endured. God's original plan for mankind is that we would never taste of the sorrow and suffering that sin would bring. *But I am saying that God can bring beauty from the ashes in your life.* His hand is not so short that He can't save you from your circumstances, or walk with you through the fire. The book of Hebrews tells us that we have a high priest who is able to sympathize with our weaknesses, and His throne is a throne of grace where we can receive mercy and help in our time of need (see 4:15–16). That's the heart of our Father. We can trust His love, even when we don't understand His ways.

Read Daniel 3:1–30.
According to this passage, what was the only thing that burned in the fire?

_____

_____

Share about a time when going through a trial helped you to leave a form of bondage behind.

_____

_____

_____

_____

_____

This story has great lessons for us about how God works through our trials. The testimony of these young men became *greater* because they went through this trial. They were instrumental in bringing many more people to the Lord through the trial than they could ever have been without it. They came out unharmed, without even smelling like smoke!

I know people like that: Although their lives have been terribly scarred, the stench of sin and suffering has been replaced with the sweet aroma of God's presence. Spending time with them is as refreshing as a walk in a garden. That's beauty from ashes.

God wants to meet us in our own fiery furnaces, so that we can experience His awesome love and power in ways we couldn't without them. He burns those things that hold us captive and accomplishes His work in us in the process.

In verses 17 and 18, these men told the king that they were sure their God was able to deliver them, but *even if He didn't,* they still would not worship the king's idol. They were willing to lay down their lives to the point of death to stay true to their God. And they probably didn't realize they had that kind of fortitude until they passed the test!

Whether we're the ones going through the trial, or we know someone else who is, these are both opportunities to share our hope in Christ with others. People can be drawn to Him just by watching us walk through hardships with a sense of peace and purpose that they wish they had.

But then there are those times when God doesn't save — at least not in the way that we want Him to. A child dies, for example; a loved one is killed in an accident; or a friend dies of cancer even after we've prayed so fervently that they would be healed. How do we explain a loving God who, though certainly able to save and heal, sometimes chooses not to?

Read Isaiah 55:8–9.

Has there ever been a time when God's ways proved to be higher than your ways? Explain. How were you blessed by this experience?

_____

_____

_____

_____

God's ways are not our ways — and they never will be. First Corinthians 13:12 tells us, *Now I know in part: then I shall know fully. . . .* By seeing the big picture, God knows exactly how each piece of the puzzles of our lives can fit together for *our* good and for *His* glory. He is the One who is in control, and we can rest assured that nothing will ever happen to us that hasn't first been filtered through the hands of our loving Father, and nothing can separate us from His love. He can turn even the worst situations around for our good.

So when we come up against things we just don't understand, we cannot go by our feelings. We must go by the facts. The storms of life don't change God's promises or His nature. When I am in a difficult situation in which I don't know what to do, I go back to the things I do know about Him: He loves me, He will work all things together for my good, and He has wonderful things planned for my life.[2]

We must place our trust in the fact that the sovereign God, the Creator of the very breath we breathe, knows what He's doing. We can let go and just let God be God. Dear friend, trust your heartaches to your loving Savior today, who alone can make all things new.

Read Job 1:1–12 and 42:5.

After considering Job's words in Job 42:5, describe how you think his experience strengthened Job's walk with God.

_____

_____

Have you ever experienced a difficult time that brought you closer to God?

_____

_____

_____

Job's story shows us that *Satan cannot test us without God's permission.* At the time, Job was one of the wealthiest men on earth; he was a family man who loved and prayed for his ten kids. He was healthy and strong, and his heart was right with God as he lived a life of excellence. But he was about to be *tested in the furnace of affliction* (Isaiah 48:10). In the space of a heartbeat, Job lost all of his wealth and possessions, his family, and his health. Most of us can't fathom that kind of suffering, and yet Job was able to worship God in the end. Amazing.

Why does God allow such tremendous hardship in some Christians' lives? I believe that, at least in Job's case, God wanted to prove him; to deepen his faith and build character in his life; and eventually bless him in the end and make him an example to us of how to walk through suffering without losing our faith. Through all of our trials, God teaches us to walk by faith. *Often we experience His awesome power best when our own strength is gone and our hearts are humble.*

"Satan looks for people to *devour;* but God looks for people to *empower.*"[3] We see this principle demonstrated in 2 Chronicles 16:9: *For the eyes of the LORD range throughout the earth to strengthen those whose hearts are fully committed to him.* We do not worship a God who delights in watching His children suffer in anguish or who ignores our despair. Instead, according to Isaiah 30:18, *the LORD longs to be gracious to you.*

God's compassion overrides our limited understanding. He desires for us to draw near to Him, overcome our struggles through faith, and be strengthened in the process. But in His mercy, God would rather we go through temporary trials that draw us close to Him now, than for us to skip happily into eternity without ever knowing Him. His love is too great to lose us forever.

Look up the following verses. According to each, what are the benefits that trials can bring into our lives?

VERSE	BENEFIT FROM TRIALS
James 1:2–4, 12	_____
2 Corinthians 4:16–18	_____
2 Corinthians 1:3–5, 8–10	_____

Our struggles are the fertile ground in which God's Word takes root, with a yield that far exceeds our own ability to produce. Struggles will produce in us obedience, character, compassion, eternal rewards, the fruit of the Spirit, the comfort we need to comfort others, and ultimately, a deeper relationship with God.

GOD WANTS US TO BE FREE!

Read Galatians 5:1, 13.

I love it when the Word of God speaks so plainly! Why did Christ set us free? So we can walk in freedom! As my kids would say, "Duh!" But as simple as that concept may seem to understand, it's a lot more challenging to actually live it out.

Much of the world thinks that Christianity is about following a bunch of rules and never having any fun again. But it is actually just the opposite. God's Word is meant to direct us *away* from the world's counterfeit "happiness," and *toward* the freedom and joy that can be found only in an intimate relationship with the heavenly Father. But we can only experience this when we live within the boundaries God has set up for our protection and growth, when we obey His Word. God has never promised us lives free from trials, but He has promised lives that can be fruitful, focused, and full of joy, regardless of the circumstances in which we find ourselves. We experience real joy by abiding in Christ and obeying what He tells us to do.

The balance of our God-given freedom is to walk in it without slipping into sin, or causing someone else to stumble. Galatians 5:13 instructs us to avoid indulging in the sinful nature. That's God's line drawn in the sand. If your "freedom" to do something could hurt a weaker brother or sister, don't do it. First Corinthians 13 tells us that if we aren't doing something out of love, we're just making noise. Let's not ruin our testimony by our careless actions.

Seven Areas in Which God Wants Us to Experience Freedom

1. Freedom from the Power of Sin

Read Romans 6:5–14.

What keys to overcoming sin can be found in these verses?

_____

_____

This is probably the number-one area most Christians struggle with — because of our sin nature. When we accept Jesus into our hearts and begin to live for Him, we do an about face to the world's motives, priorities, and ways of thinking, and we begin to follow hard after God. But everything within us has become accustomed to doing things our way, and suddenly it's supposed to change — overnight! In actuality, it's not that easy.

Overcoming sin is a gradual, lifelong process. Sanctification (or being "set apart" for God) happens as we daily choose to submit to God's authority — especially when we want one thing and God wants another! As my husband, Dave, says, "the world tells us that dying to what we want should make us miserable. But, really, as we lose our lives for Christ's sake, we find it, and find real joy in the process!"

2. FREEDOM FROM GUILT

Guilt is one of Satan's favorite weapons to keep Christians discouraged and defeated. We've all sinned, and honestly, we all continue to miss the mark too frequently — so how can we learn to live above guilt?

Read 1 John 1:8–9 and Romans 5:8–9.

According to these passages, how are we justified?

_____

_____

How could the knowledge of this help you to let go of the guilt of your past?

_____

_____

_____

_____

God has chosen to cancel our insurmountable debt to Him. Through Christ's blood, God calls us justified — and that means it's "just-as-if-I'd" never sinned! Talk about amazing grace! He has removed our sins so we can live free from guilt. The least we can for do for Him is walk in the freedom that He bought for us. When I've sinned, and I'm tempted to wallow in guilt, I ask God's forgiveness for what I've done, and then remind myself that *while we were yet sinners, Christ died for us* (Romans 5:8 NASB). When He had no guarantee I'd ever choose to serve Him, He chose to die for me, and now that I'm trying to live for Him, I can still be sure He accepts me.

3. FREEDOM FROM CONDEMNATION

Read Romans 8:1–4 and 2 Corinthians 10:3–5.

According to these passages, what sort of (or, how much) condemnation is there for Christians?

_____

_____

_____

_____

From the verses in 2 Corinthians, what key can we find to help us overcome condemnation?

_____

_____

_____

I used to wear condemnation like a nametag. It ate me alive. I couldn't worship, I couldn't read the Word, and I couldn't look in the mirror without feeling condemned for all my failures and weaknesses. Without realizing it, I had exchanged my bondage to sin for bondage to condemnation. The Bible calls Satan *the accuser of* [the] *brethren* (Revelation 12:10 NASB). He wants to steal our joy and tell us that we're nothing but big, fat losers! But he's the *father of lies* (John 8:44), and when we hear his lies whispered in our ears, we need to remind ourselves of what the Word says: When we confess our sins, He is faithful and just to forgive us and remove our sins from us as far as the east is from the west (see 1 John 1:9 and Psalm 103:12).

While it is true that God does not *condemn* us, there will be times in which the Holy Spirit will *convict* our hearts of sin. Let's look at the difference between conviction and condemnation.

CONVICTION:	CONDEMNATION:
Originates from the Holy Spirit	Originates from Satan
Deals with a specific need for change	Generalizes that everything is hopeless
Encourages us to repent and change	Offers no hope for change
Offers a specific solution to the problem	Makes us feel there are no solutions
Encourages us to *come to God* for help	Makes us want to *run from God*
Leaves us encouraged and motivated	Leaves us discouraged and unmotivated

Take it from a seasoned fighter: Guard your heart from the enemy's lies. Fill your spirit with the promises found in God's Word. If you do, it will change your life!

4. FREEDOM FROM UNFORGIVENESS AND BITTERNESS
Read Ephesians 4:31–32 and Hebrews 12:14–15.

According to these passages of Scripture, why should we forgive?

_____

_____

What happens when we become bitter?

_____

_____

How can we overcome bitterness in our lives?

_____

_____

Unforgiveness can be crippling to Christians. When we're seething mad toward someone, are we experiencing freedom or bondage? Is that person paying the price for what they've done, or are we, as we're bound up with anger and unforgiveness? We are! And when we release our hurts to God and forgive that person, we are the ones who are set free! God's way is exactly opposite from the world's way of handling things.

In order to truly forgive someone else, we must first understand the magnitude of God's forgiveness toward us. Matthew 18 tells about a slave who owed his master the equivalent of what would today be millions of dollars; there was no way the slave would ever be able to repay his master. _We too owed a debt that we could never pay._ Realizing how much we've been forgiven gives us the power to forgive others. _While we were yet sinners_ (Romans 5:8 NASB), God chose to make the way possible for our forgiveness — He didn't wait until He felt that we were acting sorry enough to please Him! He took the first step when we owed a debt that would separate us from Him forever. He even modeled for us the ultimate forgiveness when He forgave from the cross those who knew not what they did (see Luke 23:34), and through His grace and power, we can now also forgive those who hurt us.

It works like this: A breach in a horizontal relationship with someone on earth causes a breach in our vertical relationship with our heavenly Father. Matthew 6:14 and 15 says it plainly: When we don't forgive, He doesn't forgive us! We can't hear His direction, because He won't speak until we've put out the fires of unforgiveness that we keep stoking in our hearts! We _must_ forgive, through the grace of God; then He will forgive us, and we are set free!

Bitterness is the fruit of unforgiveness. When it's allowed to grow, it yields a plentiful harvest like a well-cared-for plant. Bitterness is like unforgiveness multiplied by 100, and it will not only destroy _us,_ the Word says that it will _defile many_ (Hebrews 12:15). How many marriages have ended because one spouse refused to forgive, and the bitterness that resulted "defiled many"?

There was a time in my life when I was extremely bitter toward Dave. He was traveling a lot with his job while I stayed home with our children who were toddlers at the time, and I resented it. When a godly older woman pointed out that "there needed to be some forgiveness in my life," (and I thought I was hiding it!), I realized just how bitter I was. For days I fought it, crying out to the Lord, realizing that Dave's schedule wasn't likely to change. Yet just three weeks after I finally made the choice to forgive him and let go of my bitter attitude, Dave was offered a promotion and a position in which he was required to travel much less!

I am convinced that my bitterness was holding back God's blessing. When I released my anger to God, the clog in the pipe was finally cleared. Unforgiveness costs us way more than it's worth. No matter how much it may seem to be hurting you, repent, give your bitterness to God, and let Him deal with it. *Life is too short to let your past ruin your future.*

5. FREEDOM FROM FEAR

Read 2 Timothy 1:7 and Isaiah 41:9–10.

According to 2 Timothy 1:7, what three tools has God given us to overcome our fear, and how are we to use them?

_____

_____

_____

_____

List any promises given in Isaiah 41:9–10.

_____

_____

_____

What is God asking you to trust Him with today?

_____

_____

_____

_____

What are you afraid of? I have battled fear my whole life so I am a seasoned soldier in this area. Satan has a whole arsenal of fears especially designed to discourage and disable women, keeping us at a safe distance from God's exciting plan for us. For many of us, as soon as God begins to speak to our hearts about His plan and purpose for us, fear begins to echo in our hearts like thunder.

But there is one good thing about fear: *Fear brings us to a crossroads where we must choose to stand on God's Word and take that thought captive, or give up and let the devil win. Satan is a liar.* But he also knows that when we overcome fear, we become lethal to the kingdom of darkness, and so he does his best to keep us held tightly in fear's grip. But *through Christ* we can live above our fears and fulfill God's plan for our lives.

As misunderstood as I may be by saying this, I believe that pride is hiding at the root of fear. Fear is really a form of self-preservation, which in some contexts can actually be a good thing when it alerts us to very real dangers in the world. But when fear becomes a form of selfishness and a means to protect our own interests, we must remember that God calls us to die to what we want and place our trust in Him. *When I allow fear to dictate my actions, God is not in the center of my world. I am!* But when fear rears its ugly head and I give it over to God, He helps me step past my fear and walk in victory.

Did you catch that? Our fears don't necessarily go away, but He helps us *overcome* them through faith. And it really works! My life has changed dramatically since realizing: (1) My fear is not an excuse to disobey God, and (2) All the power I need to defeat fear in my life is found only *in Christ alone.*

6. FREEDOM FROM THE WORLD'S MINDSET
Read 1 John 2:15–17 and Romans 12:1–2.
According to 1 John 2:17, how does following the will of God surpass following the ways of the world?

_____

_____

According to Romans 12, what changes us? What will we know when we obey Him?

_____

_____

What are some practical ways in which you can renew your mind this week?

_____

_____

_____

Satan loves to tempt Christians with the four P's: power, possessions, position, and pleasure.[4] Although these things are not "evil" in and of themselves, when they become our sole or most important focus, our spiritual life suffers. And even though many of us would never say so out loud, we tend to think that these four P's can bring us happiness. First Timothy gives us a higher standard, saying that godliness and contentment are worthier goals, and that if we have food and clothing, we should be content (6:6–8). Wow! Does that go against American culture, or what? Yet how many people in the world don't even have food or clothing? Let's never forget how blessed we truly are.

Nobody's going to pull up to heaven's gates with a U-haul! All of the possessions we've slaved so hard to buy on this earth will be worthless when we get there. The power, pleasure, or position we managed to achieve here on earth won't mean a thing in heaven. Granted, God loves us and wants to meet our needs and bless us abundantly, but He never wants us to waste our lives pursuing things.

There's a bumper sticker that says, "He who dies with the most toys wins." Unfortunately, that seems to be the primary way of thinking in America! But as the true saying goes, "Only one life, twill soon be past, Only what's done for Christ will last." We do well to live with eternity in mind.

7. FREEDOM TO BE ORGANIZED.

Read Philippians 1:6 and Ephesians 5:15–17.

According to the Philippians passage, who will help you fulfill God's will, and what promise is given to encourage us?

_____

_____

_____

From the passage in Ephesians, what four things will help us use our time wisely?

_____

_____

I like the way Philippians 1:6 reads in The Living Bible: *I am sure that God who began the good work within you will keep right on helping you grow in his grace until his task within you is finally finished on that day when Jesus Christ returns.* It's not all up to us! We have an almighty God within us who can teach us how to use our time wisely. The Holy Spirit can be our organizational mentor if we'll ask for His help.

God knows everything we have to get done, day in and day out, and He knows how to get it all accomplished. Just look at all Jesus accomplished while He was on earth, and He was never frazzled! *Our effectiveness in God's work is a direct result of how we invest our time, whether in futile things or in seeking first the kingdom of God.*

A very practical way to get organized is to learn to live by a datebook or a palm pilot. Mine contains every detail of my life, from my daily calendar to birthdays to addresses to grocery lists! It's my lifeline. It holds my long-term and short-term goals, my plans for upcoming events, and my budget. With everything in one place, even I can get a handle on things.

This combination of learning to be led by God's Spirit in my *heart* and a system of organization for my head *helps* me stay focused on the things God wants me to do, even on the craziest days!

How to Stay Free

Although we weren't exactly "born free" like the song says, we can choose to stay free by staying close to God. We can learn to be content and at peace since God is ultimately in control of our lives. We can be free from the pursuit of worldly wealth and possessions, realizing that this life is just a preview of coming attractions, and we can allow God to work in our lives daily, as we set aside time to pray, study His Word, and meditate on what He's teaching us.

We can replace old bad habits and thoughts with new godly ones as we abide in Christ. And we can stay encouraged and lifted up, following the model of the early church by spending time with other Christians — eating, praying, and praising God together. As we stay connected with God and other believers in a church that teaches God's Word, He will keep us on His path and provide us with all that we need to serve Him with excellence.

As Pastor Mark Balmer says, "Do the right thing today, and tomorrow will take care of itself."[5] As we abandon ourselves to the will and purposes of God and walk in His strength, He will give us the power to overcome every obstacle. *You can do whatever God calls you to do, for greater is He that is in you than he that is in the world! Just trust God, and watch Him do His thing through you!*

PRAYER

Thank You that You're in control of my life, Lord, and that You have the power to help me overcome every obstacle designed to hold me back. Help me learn from the trials You've allowed in my life, and to choose to stand firm in Your amazing love. I choose to believe what Your Word says is true about me. Strengthen me for the task that You want me to do, Lord. I put my trust in You. Amen.

SUMMARY POINTS

• God will empower us to do whatever He calls us to do.

• God allows us to go through trials to draw us closer to Him and to build character in our lives.

• God wants us to walk in freedom over anything that would entangle us.

• The Holy Spirit is our Teacher, and He will guide us in God's plan and purpose for our lives.

FROM PRINT TO POWER:
PERSONAL APPLICATION

1. Look back over this chapter and summarize your thoughts and feelings about the material that was presented.

_____
_____
_____
_____
_____
_____
_____
_____

2. How do you believe that God wants you to act on what you've learned?

_____
_____
_____
_____
_____
_____
_____
_____

3. Are you going through a trial right now that God is allowing in order to teach you something? What might God want you to learn from this experience?

_____
_____
_____
_____
_____
_____
_____
_____
_____

4. Which areas of freedom discussed in this chapter spoke most directly to your heart? What did you learn about yourself, and what freedoms do you need to experience more fully? What can you do this week to make those freedoms a reality in your life?

_____

_____

_____

_____

_____

_____

_____

_____

_____

_____

_____

_____

_____

THE PRIZE

SECTION THREE

CHAPTER 11

STEPPING OUT OF THE BOAT:
FINDING YOUR PLACE TO SERVE

"You did not choose me, but I chose you and appointed you to go and bear fruit — fruit that will last."

— John 15:16

Imagine with me a day in your future. Your time on earth has been completed, and you suddenly find yourself in heaven. There before you stands the judgment seat of Christ, and excited and nervous, you realize you're about to meet your Savior face to face. It's all so wonderful . . . so amazing . . . so incredible . . .

You suddenly notice that none of the earthly treasures you worked so hard to accumulate in your lifetime are anywhere in sight — they are meaningless now. So you begin to take a mental inventory of how you spent your life. Did you serve God with your whole heart? Did you honor Him with your time, your talents, and your treasure? Did you take the time to truly love others the way His Word instructed? Did you make a difference in the lives of other people? And most importantly, did you bring anyone to heaven with you?

What if that scenario happened to you today? What will be left when the wood, hay, and stubble of your life is burned away? What works, done in secret, will be rewarded openly? *What will you have to offer the One who left the wonders of heaven to die on a cross for you?* If your whole life on earth were boiled down to this one moment, what would be left?

Share your own thoughts about what it will be like to meet Jesus face to face.

_____

_____

_____

_____

How does thinking about that future moment challenge and inspire you?

_____

_____

_____

THE HEART OF A SERVANT

There's a bumper sticker that reads, "Jesus is coming soon. Look busy!" But truly living for God is hardly about just looking busy. It's not about building our own reputation, claiming the spotlight for ourselves, or using someone else's weakness to make us look more spiritual. Serving God is about the _privilege_ of giving back to the very One who gives us our breath each day! It's about finding what we're called to do and working alongside the almighty God to accomplish His will and expand His kingdom. It's letting Him call the shots in our lives and serving Him from the overflow of His love in our hearts. _It's all about love!_

GOD'S AGENDA, NOT OURS

Read Matthew 20:20–28.

According to verse 28, why did Jesus come to earth?

_____

What did Jesus say makes a person great? In contrast, what was this mother's goal for her sons?

_____

_____

What can you learn about your own attitude about serving Christ from these examples?

_____

_____

_____

_____

_____

Any mom can see the human nature in this woman's heart. She was proud of her boys, and she wanted the world to know! Don't we feel the same way about our kids? Why else do we have bumper stickers that say, "My child is an honor student at Better-Than-You Elementary!"? Or, "My kid beat up your honor student!" One way or another most of us will find a way to brag about our kids!

But this well-meaning mom missed the point. I can just picture Jesus' gentle response as He explained to her that position and honor aren't what life is about, that the important stuff isn't up to us anyway! Life is about doing the *Father's* will, not ours, serving *Him* however He asks.

We don't fit God into our agenda; we fit into His. *We don't add Him to our lives like we would a hobby. He **is** our life!* This universe is His backyard, not ours, so we let Him decide what to do. No one calls the president of the United States and tells him what committee he'd like to chair for him. That would be crazy! The president *appoints* people to do certain things, and it would be an honor to be thought worthy to serve him.

We have an opportunity of much grander proportions! We're "God-appointees." Yet how many times do we think, *I think I'll do such and such for God.* If it's in His plan, He'll bless it, but if it's just what we want to do, we're on our own, left to attempt the work of the Spirit in the strength of the flesh. It won't work! As the King of the universe, He invites us to join Him in His eternal plan. Let's look at two such appointments.

Read Jeremiah 1:4–10.
What did God assign Jeremiah to do?

_____

How did God make His plans clear to him?

_____

_____

Has there ever been a time when God spoke clear, specific direction to you? Share your experience.

_____

_____

_____

WHAT SHOULD I DO?

Once we've decided that God wants us to be busy serving Him, what is our next step? How can we know exactly what God wants us to do? Should we just commit to the first opportunity that presents itself? Can we assume that God wants us to jump into the things we're good at? Or do we wait to hear God speak to us like He did to Charlton Heston in *The Ten Commandments*? Who can forget that voice: "Moses . . . MOSES!" If you wait to hear a voice like that split the heavens, you'll be waiting awhile! The real question to ask is: How did Jesus know how to serve the Father? *What would Jesus do, anyway?*

Let's take a look at the Word and find out.

Read John 5:19–20 and 12:25–26.

How is it possible for us to "see" what the Father was doing like Jesus did?

_____

_____

What does "hating" our lives here on earth have to do with serving God and learning to hear His voice?

_____

_____

What can we learn from verse 26 about knowing where God wants us to serve?

_____

_____

_____

Henry Blackaby and Claude V. King, authors of *Experiencing God,* write:

> Because He loves you and wants to involve you in His work, He will show you where He is working so you can join Him. . . . Jesus watched to see where the Father was at work. When He saw, He did what He saw the Father doing. . . . When you see the Father at work around you, that is your invitation to adjust your life to Him and join Him in that work.[1]

They continue, "The scriptures tell us of some things only God can do. You need to learn to identify these. Then, when something happens around you that only God can do, you can know it is God's activity."[2]

THINGS ONLY GOD CAN DO

What are these things that only God can do? Here are several:

• God draws people to Himself.

• God causes people to seek after Him.

• God reveals spiritual truth.

• God convicts the world of guilt regarding sin.

• God convicts the world of righteousness.

• God convicts the world of judgment.[3]

SERVING GOD BRINGS HIM GLORY

Read Matthew 5:14–16 and John 17:4.

What two things did Jesus say about His work on earth?

_____

_____

Who deserves the glory when we allow God to do His work through us?

_____

_____

What has God called you to do or to complete for Him?

_____

_____

If you let your light shine *in such a way that they may see your good works, and glorify your Father* (Matthew 5:16 NASB), then *He* gets glory from what you do! People are drawn to God when they see Him using ordinary people to do extraordinary things. Serving God is about both what He does through us, and what we do for Him.

Do you remember the crowd's reaction to Peter and John when they challenged the religious leaders? According to Acts 4:13, *when they saw the courage of Peter and John and realized that they were unschooled, ordinary men, they were astonished and they took note that these men had been with Jesus.* When we do what God calls us to do, especially when it's beyond our capabilities, people will see we've been with Jesus, too!

The crowd was drawn to God's presence in the disciples' lives. Who *they* were didn't really matter. The crowd was drawn to Jesus, not *them.* Do you get that? The key is not who we are, or what God asks us to do, but that His name is lifted up! That happens when we serve when, where, and how God wants us to.

If I were to sing a song in order to receive compliments from other people, I might as well stuff a sock in it! But if I sing in order to draw people to God, then He gets the glory. Sometimes we throw the baby out with the bathwater, thinking, *If I sing or minister in front of other people, I'm full of pride.* Sometimes you could be! But if that type of ministry is what God has directed you to do, then you would be arrogant to *not* do it! Which leads us to our next hurdle: fear.

The Courage and Power to Obey

What if you're scared of what God might want you to do? Guess what? That's normal! Most people experience fear when they do something new. Do you remember the twelve leaders whom Moses sent to spy out the Promised Land? God had already promised the land to them, but when they saw the circumstances, they were afraid. Ten of the twelve leaders walked in fear instead of in faith, and they missed out on the promise of God because of it. Most of us can relate to their fear. Even the apostle Paul said he experienced *fear and much trembling* in his work for God (1 Corinthians 2:3). If you're scared, welcome to the club — you're in good company!

Even still, fear is not an excuse for disobeying God. If what He calls us to do makes us nervous — especially if it scares us to death — then too often we decline, thinking that surely the omnipotent God must have gotten the wrong address! But what glory does He get from our cowering in fear? *True humility obeys. False humility hides behind what people will think of us. The heart of a servant obeys without question or excuse.* Let's remind ourselves what the Bible has to say about fear.

Read 2 Timothy 1:7.

According to this verse, what *didn't* God give us?

_____

What three things *did* He give us — things that we so desperately need to do His work?

1. The _____ to accomplish it.

2. The _____ to care enough to do it.

3. The _____ to be smart enough to get it done!

If fear doesn't come from God, where does it come from, and why?

_____

_____

How has fear held you back at times from doing what you feel led to do?

_____

_____

Read Exodus 2–3.

Moses had lots of reasons to be shaking in his boots, or should I say sandals! There he was, minding his own business, hanging out in the wilderness with a bunch of sheep. He was incognito — hiding from his past and probably plenty frustrated with his future. Once he had been a highly regarded son to the most powerful man on earth, living in the lap of luxury. But now he found himself in a blue-collar job, seemingly destined to finish his life on the back forty.

He'd blown it big time, and that defeat probably played over and over in his mind on a daily basis. He had killed a man and hid the body, thinking no one had seen him. But then he was found out, and now the only father figure he had ever known wanted him dead. So Moses had hit the road, and hit rock bottom.

Think about that. Moses was a murderer hiding out in the wilderness. From a human standpoint, it seemed as if his chance to be used by God had passed, don't you think? Ever been there? I have. Have you ever thought that because of your past surely God could never use you in the future? Like Paul Harvey says, let's hear *the rest of the story!*

God's heart was breaking for His people in Egypt, and He had a plan to deliver them. So *in spite of Moses' failures,* God paid him a little visit. He was about to take Moses from the back forty to the front lines, and, like us, Moses was convinced there'd been a mistake!

Read Exodus 3:1–12; 4:10–16.

For the first nine verses of their visit Moses thought God's plan sounded good — until he heard his own name. Suddenly he thought there had been a mistake! *No way, God!* he must have thought. *Don't you know I'm a loser? Weren't You watching when I ruined my life? Besides, Lord, I stutter, I don't have a clue what to say, no one will believe me, and I know I'm the wrong guy for the job! So, please find someone that's more qualified than me!*

Can you relate? When God comes knocking at our doors, it can be scary for us, too, especially when what He asks us to do requires extra courage and faith!

According to Exodus 3:10, who had come up with this plan: God or Moses?

_____

Who should come up with the plans for your life?

_____

From verses 11 and 12, what was Moses' reaction to God's invitation, and how did God reply?

_____

_____

In Exodus 4:10–14, as Moses again tried to talk God out of His plan, how did God prove that Moses' weaknesses wouldn't be a problem?

_____

_____

And in verse 14, what was God's reaction to Moses' hesitation, and how did He solve the problem?

_____

_____

_____

What does this passage teach you about the things God has spoken to you regarding your own life?

_____

_____

_____

_____

DISTRIBUTORS, NOT MANUFACTURERS

Often we shrink back from doing what God wants us to do because we misunderstand, thinking that we have to do it in our own strength, and we know that we can't.

In his book, *On Being a Servant of God,* author Warren Wiersbe explains,

> The trouble with too many of us is that we think God called us to be manufacturers when He really called us to be distributors. He alone has the resources to meet human needs; all we can do is receive His riches and share them with others. "Silver and gold I do not have," Peter announced, "but what I do have I give you" (Acts 3:6). When it comes to ministry, all of us are bankrupt, and only God is rich. . . . So one of the first steps we must take before our service can be used of God is to confess our bankruptcy and receive by faith the grace that we need for acceptable service.[4]

Can you see how this takes the pressure off of us to be able to do the impossible in our own strength? It's *God's* work in us, not *our* work for Him that will get the job done![5]

Read Ephesians 3:20.

How does this passage encourage you to think "outside the box" of your limitations?

_____

_____

_____

_____

What are some things that God has empowered you to do that you could never have done without Him?

_____

_____

_____

The question then is not, "are you able?" but, "are you willing?" when the Master calls.

SERVING GOD THROUGH OUR GIFTS

Read 1 Corinthians 13:9–12 and John 4:34–36.

How much of what God is doing can we understand at this time?

_____

_____

According to this passage in John, what tells us about God's will for us?

_____

_____

I like to think of God's will as a giant puzzle. How amazing it is that God can fit all the pieces of all the puzzles of all our lives together to create His masterpiece! My own tiny piece of God's puzzle is to simply follow and obey Him, allowing Him to make my life into something useful and beautiful for His kingdom.

CREATED FOR A PURPOSE

This is where our unique gifts come in. The Bible tells us that we've each been given specific gifts, like tools, to help us do the work God has for us. _Our part is to find out which gifts we've received, determine what He is calling us to do, and then diligently put our gifts to work to accomplish those things._

Think of it this way. If I were a computer engineer who needed a computer model that could do one certain type of task, I would create one with those specific capabilities, rather than settling for a generic model. _Just like that computer, we've been custom designed from_ *our conception with a specific purpose in mind!* Don't be alarmed if you don't *feel* able to do what God calls you to do. You're not! It will be His work in you, not your own efforts, that will make the difference. The Holy Spirit lives in us to be our Helper, and He's on call 24/7!

Read Romans 12:4–8.

In the space below, list the gifts that are discussed in this passage.

1._____
2._____
3._____
4._____
5._____
6._____
7._____

What are some ways in which you've seen these gifts in operation?

_____
_____

Is there a function listed here that you feel could be yours?

_____
_____

According to Ephesians 2:10, what are we created to do?

_____

What do we know about these good works?

_____
_____

Is there a "good work" to which you feel you have been called? If so, what is it?

_____
_____
_____
_____

STEWARDS OF GOD'S GIFTS

First Peter 4:10–11 tells us that *as each one has received a special gift, employ it in serving one another, as good stewards of the manifold grace of God . . . whoever serves, let him do so as by the strength which God supplies; so that in all things God may be glorified through Jesus Christ* (NASB). Let's take a look at the following words from the text so that we can clearly understand its message:

1. *Each* of us has received at least one gift from God.
2. They are *gifts,* not something we're supposed to "muster up" on our own.
3. We need to *employ* them. This will involve hard work and diligence.
4. They are to be used in *serving others*, not promoting ourselves.
5. We need to be good *stewards* of God's gifts. They're on loan to us from God.
6. We are to use them in *God's strength,* not our own.

We present ourselves to God's service — everything we are, and everything we're not — as an act of thanksgiving and stewardship, and let Him use us for His glory. Ephesians 4:16 tells us that *the whole body, being fitted and held together by that which every joint supplies, according to the proper working of each individual part, causes the growth of the body for the building up of itself in love* (NASB). Every joint is supposed to work — and we're those joints! No matter where you're at in life or what your abilities, God can use your gifts to spread His love and meet needs.

I know a lady who doesn't feel qualified to do anything "spiritual," but she is an experienced hairstylist. So when God laid it on her heart to serve the body of Christ, she volunteered to cut hair for single moms and their families at church for free once a month. Another stylist heard about it and wanted to help. Soon a shop owner wanted to join in, and now six stylists use this woman's shop one Sunday afternoon a month (when they're not open) and happily cut hair for free! *The point is, we're not all called to teach Bible studies, but we are all called to use our gifts to serve others!*

We seek God for our part in His plan — large or small, in the public eye or behind the scenes, cutting hair or sweeping up afterwards — and step by step He reveals His specific plan for us. Then we choose to accept His plan with every bit of hard work that it entails, and deliberately bypass the time wasters that try to entangle us. By doing this, we make ourselves available to be used by God in new and exciting ways. It's God's recipe for adventure! Life is never boring when you're stepping out in faith.

REACHING THE LOST FOR CHRIST

How can we prepare ourselves to be used of God? Can we just show up, or are there things we can be doing now if we don't know exactly what God wants us to do in the future? Let's find out!

Read John 9:4.

Why should we have an urgency to share our faith?

_____

_____

How do current world events support this passage of scripture?

_____

_____

_____

PREPARING OURSELVES TO BE USEFUL FOR GOD

1. INVEST TIME IN PRAYER AND STUDYING GOD'S WORD.

Second Timothy 2:15 instructs us to *do your best to present yourself to God as one approved, a workman who does not need to be ashamed and who correctly handles the word of truth.* Spending time in the Word and in prayer is where we will receive God's direction, motivation, strength, and anointing to carry out His will. Don't ever shorten that time when you feel overwhelmed — that's when you need it the most!

2. BE DILIGENT AND TENACIOUS.

The book of Proverbs stresses the importance of diligence: Without it, we'll fall short every time. Serving God almost always involves some hard work! Look at Jesus in the Garden: He sweat drops of blood as He contemplated carrying out God's will.

God's plan will often require us to move outside of *our* ability and into *His,* especially when everything within us screams, "I can't do this!" That's when we need to hold on to the word God has spoken to us like a bulldog holds on to a bone! Don't let go for anything or anybody, and if you fall, get right back in there and keep fighting! We have an enemy who wants to cut us off at every pass, but don't let him. *Hone your skills, exercise your gifts, guard your time and your heart from mediocrity, do everything with excellence, and be diligent to finish. As you do, God will be glorified!*

3. Keep a positive attitude.

The Scripture says that *the joy of the LORD is your strength* (Nehemiah 8:10). So what happens when we get down? The strength leaks out of us like air from a leaky tire. But when we stay built up, like the woman of Proverbs 31, we can smile at our future. We can choose to feed on the promises of God, and cast our cares on God. We can't change our circumstances, but we can trust that God allowed them for a purpose, and according to Romans 8:28, He will work them together for our good!

4. Choose to believe.

No matter what — *no matter what* — choose to believe in the promises of God more than what others say about you. Even in the face of great opposition, we can choose to believe. Remember, nothing is too difficult for God! Luke 1:45 tells us Mary's reaction when she learned of God's impossible task for her: *Blessed is she who has believed that what the Lord has said to her will be accomplished.* No matter what they say, you believe God, and He'll use you!

5. Forget what lies behind.

One of my favorite scriptures tells us of the apostle Paul's key to success. Once a murderer and a zealous persecutor of the church, Paul later said, *Forgetting what is behind and straining toward what is ahead, I press on toward the goal to win the prize for which God has called me heavenward in Christ Jesus* (Philippians 3:13–14). He realized that in order to move forward with God, he couldn't let his past ruin his future. He was a new creation, as we are, and he walked boldly in that forgiveness.

Don't believe the enemy's lie that you're damaged merchandise. The only way we can be disqualified from being used by God is if we walk away from His commandments, and even then, if we truly repent, He offers us a fresh start. He's the God of second chances, and His mercies are new every morning.

6. BE FAITHFUL IN THE SMALL THINGS.

The Bible says that he who is faithful in the small things will be ruler over much (see Matthew 25:23). One of God's key principles throughout His Word is faithfulness. Just as they say in the Nike ads, when God calls us to do something, come hell or high water, we should "just do it!"

Like the rewards given in the parable of the talents, our faithfulness will bring great blessings. In that parable, the servants who carefully carried out their master's orders heard these words: *"Well done, good and faithful servant! You have been faithful with a few things; I will put you in charge of many things. Come and share your master's happiness!"* (Matthew 25:23). Details do matter. Just as God told Joshua, let's *"be careful to do everything written in* [His Word]. *Then you will be prosperous and successful"* (Joshua 1:8).

7. HONE YOUR SKILLS.

Nothing bugs me more than to attend a Christian event of some sort, only to find that the performers or musicians haven't practiced, or the whole thing is sloppy, unorganized, and far below par! Is that any way to serve the King of kings? Does that make nonbelievers say, "Gee, I sure want to be like them!"? Hardly! *"Sloppy agape" is an embarrassment to God's kingdom.*

The Scriptures are full of encouragement to do things with excellence, as a testimony of the power of God within us. Colossians 3:23 tells us, *Whatever you do, work at it with all your heart, as working for the Lord, not for men.* Ecclesiastes 10:10 says that *skill will bring success.* Proverbs 22:29 also echoes that sentiment: *Do you see a man skilled in his work? He will serve before kings.* Do these verses describe slackers? No, they describe Christ's holy ambassadors who are busy doing everything they can to exalt His name. He is worthy of our best efforts, every time!

8. WALK HUMBLY WITH YOUR GOD.

Numbers 12:3 describes Moses as *more humble than anyone else on the face of the earth.* Wouldn't that be a great thing to be said about us? I find that particularly amazing when I realize that Moses was also one of the most challenged and most mightily used men in history! God stretched Moses' faith over and over again, and rather than walking in pride, Moses acknowledged how big God was, especially in the face of his own weaknesses.

When God uses us to do anything, the glory belongs to Him. I sometimes imagine a huge mirror in front of me, and when compliments come my way, I just tip that mirror up to God and give *Him* the praise, for *apart from Him we can do nothing* (John 15:5). Micah 6:8 asks and answers the question, *What does the LORD require of you? To act justly and to love mercy and to walk humbly with your God."* First Peter 5:6 says, *Humble yourselves, therefore, under God's mighty hand, that he may lift you up in due time.* Faithfulness is our part; promotion is His. When God uses you, never forget it's not about you; it's about Him!

9. LIVE FOR GOD WITH YOUR WHOLE HEART.

As the saying goes, we may be the only Bible some people will ever read. If that's the case, what kind of impression are you making? Are you prepared? Prayed up? Knowledgeable in the Word? Do you look nice? How's your hair? Your makeup? Your weight? Your breath? How about your witness in the community? Are you honest? Do you pay your bills? Do you talk behind other people's backs?

These may sound like picky questions, but these issues are all part of making a good first impression as a Christian. We don't want anything in our lives to push people away from Christ. We're serving the King of kings, and He is worth whatever effort it requires to give Him our best!

10. TAKE A LEAP OF FAITH!

Here's where the rubber meets the road! I've heard it said that God lovingly guides us to the edge of a cliff and then give us a gentle shove . . . to be able to watch us fly! We'll never know the awesome power of God until we experience it firsthand. And that won't happen if we insist on staying in our comfort zones!

Think about Peter. If he'd never taken that step out of the boat, he'd never have learned that he could walk on water! Sure, he started to sink, but Jesus was right there to save him. That must have taken raw courage and every bit of faith he could muster to step out of a boat in the middle of a storm. But it also helped him realize he was walking hand in hand with the Master of the universe!

The same is true for us. God may call us to leave behind those things we hang on to for security, and follow Him. It might be a paycheck, our parents or the hometown we love, the career we've worked so hard to attain, or a lifestyle we thought was so important. We may feel like we're sweating drops of blood along with Jesus as we persevere through trials on our way to victory. But if we'll just step out of the boat, Jesus will be right there to hold us up! He'll protect us from the storms of life as He accomplishes His supernatural work through us.

From this list of ten steps on preparing to be useful to God, which ones speak to you? In what way?

_____

_____

_____

_____

LIVES HANG IN THE BALANCE

This whole chapter boils down to this one point: *When we stand before God, He'll look at what we've done, and whom we've won.* Do you remember the puzzle we talked about earlier? Sometimes the pieces in our lives don't make much sense to us from where we are right now, but that's because we can't see the picture on the front of the box. Do you know what it is? It's a picture of the harvest! Luke 19:10 tells us, *For the Son of Man came to seek and to save what was lost.* One way or another, everything God asks us to do will fit into His divine plan to redeem mankind.

Read 1 Peter 3:15 and Matthew 9:37–38.
What are some ways in which you can be prepared to share the gospel with someone when God opens the door?

_____

_____

_____

God strategically places us in our neighborhoods, our jobs, and our social circles to carry out His will. He uses both the good and the difficult things in our lives to reach out to those who don't know Him. *The Scriptures tell us that God even allows some things to occur in our lives so we can effectively extend the comfort we've received from Him to others.* People are drawn to Christ as they see us go through difficulties with peace and a sense of purpose.

In their book, *How to Talk about Jesus Without Freaking Out,* authors Jim and Karen Covell and Victoria Michaels Rogers have the following to say:

> Everyone understands failure. . . . What people want to know is: Is your faith there for you even when you blow it? Is it truly part of your life, or is it just a passing phase like last year's trendy diet? What people are looking for is something that will be there for them even if they fail.[6]

Together they have come up with a painless way to introduce the gospel into your conversation:

> We have a simple way to remember what we believe is the most effective approach to witnessing. We call them three stories: their story, your story, and His story. Learning their story — a person's life story, or even just the story of his spiritual journey — is what earns you the right to then tell your story — how you met Jesus — and finally His story — God's plan of salvation.[7]

One Shot to Influence Others for Eternity

Consider this sobering thought: Someday this life will end, and the people we've rubbed shoulders with over the years will either join us for an eternity of joy with God, or be forever separated from His love. *As the door to eternity begins to close, many lives hang in the balance.* Sharing God's love and His plan of salvation is the most important thing we can ever do. When we don't share, it's like sitting on a billion dollars while the world around us starves. Aren't you glad someone swallowed their own fears to share the gospel with you? Where would you be today without Jesus?

When all is said and done and we stand before our Savior's throne, I pray we will have used our gifts and our lives to connect people with their heavenly Father. If we have, then we'll hear those precious words, *"Well done, good and faithful servant"* (Matthew 25:21). Our willingness to take a deep breath and step out of the boat can change a life for eternity.

PRAYER

Father, I am humbled as I think that You loved me enough to pursue me even when I didn't want anything to do with You. I pray that I can take what I've learned today and apply it to my life. I offer myself to You afresh today. Have Thine own way, Lord. Let Your will be done in my life, through Your grace and power. In Jesus' name I pray. Amen.

SUMMARY POINTS

- Our works for God will be worth their cost when we stand before Christ.
- God will give us the courage and the power to do His will.
- We will be held accountable for how we use God's gifts to us.
- Sharing our faith is a part of every Christian's calling.

FROM PRINT TO POWER:
PERSONAL APPLICATION

1. Go back to the page on which we listed the gifts of the Holy Spirit (page 207). Do you see one that's evident in your life? Begin to seek God for how He wants to use your gifts in His plan.

_____

_____

_____

_____

2. Think back over the things you've felt God has asked you to do over the years. Is there something you've been putting off, or still need to finish? Is there a skill on which He wants you to work that you've put on the back burner? Pray about these things, and then do what you feel He is directing you to do.

_____

_____

_____

_____

_____

_____

3. Spend some time thinking about your testimony, and then write it down. When you're done, see if you can shorten it to a few minutes. Then daily ask God to open doors for you to share your story, and watch Him work!

_____

_____

_____

_____

_____

_____

_____

CHAPTER 12

COME AWAY, MY BELOVED:
A CALL TO
DISCIPLESHIP

"My beloved is mine, and I am his."
— Song of Songs 2:16 NASB

As we begin the last chapter of this study, we find ourselves at a defining moment. We are ready to answer the critical question: Will we choose to live for ourselves, or truly live to fulfill God's purposes? Will we be complacent or compelled, stepping back in fear or stepping forward in faith? *My friend, true balance in our lives comes only as we keep our eyes fixed on the Cross, for only then can God make a difference through us for eternity.*

How meaningful are Jesus' words to us today from Matthew 11:28–30:

> *"Come to me, all you who are weary and burdened, and I will give you rest. Take my yoke upon you and learn from me, for I am gentle and humble in heart, and you will find rest for your souls. For my yoke is easy and my burden is light."*

His gentle call has not changed. He still woos us to an ever-deepening relationship with Him. How different from the frantic lifestyles we keep! And yet, even on the busiest of days, we can find "rest for our souls" as we come to Him.

Do you think this kind of "rest" is really possible in today's culture?

_____

How do you personally find "rest for your soul" in the midst of chaotic days, or in adverse circumstances?

_____

_____

• **We can rest in Christ's completed work at the cross.** Our salvation is bought and paid for. We can never earn it. It's a gift that was purchased with the precious blood of the Lamb of God — for us — for *you,* and no matter what, the world can never take that gift away.

• **We can rest in God's protective care.** He's the almighty God, sovereign and unchanging, and His hosts of angels are all around us to keep us safe.

• **We can rest in His ability to accomplish His work in us.** Although we can never do His work in our own natural abilities, God provides us with His supernatural strength and ability to carry out His plan. He will never ask us to do something without providing the resources that we need.

• **We can rest in His provision for our future.** As a believer, you are the apple of God's eye, and His Word promises that your future is in His hands. Jeremiah 29:11 tells us that He knows the plans He has for us, plans to prosper us and not harm us, plans to give us hope and a future. We need never worry when God's in control!

• **We can rest in His incredible love for us.** *For God so loved the world that he gave his one and only Son* (John 3:16). Beyond description and measurement, God's love for us is deeper than the deepest ocean and as sure as tomorrow's sunrise. Nothing can separate us from His love!

Read Psalm 116:5–9.

What words does this passage use to portray God's character? How do these verses minister to you in whatever situation you find yourself in today?

_____

_____

_____

_____

_____

_____

_____

MOVING FORWARD IN GOD'S REST

With these issues settled in our hearts, we can move forward from a position of God's rest, as we decide where to *move ahead* and what to *leave behind*. This is where balance can make us and unbalance can break us! With balance, our lives can run smoothly, as we live with a plan to maintain our priorities. But without it, our lives and our testimonies soon get thrown out of whack as we desperately try to please man rather than please God. When we attempt to live this way, God's direction and peace are lost in the process. I know this from experience! We pay a high price when we plan our days according to our agenda rather than God's.

As we conclude this study, let's take a few minutes to review what God has spoken to us throughout the last few weeks — as well as where we are and where we are headed. My prayer is that these truths that have been shared have jumped off of the pages of this study and into your heart.

HOW ARE YOU DOING?

• **Your relationship with God**
How do you feel God is encouraging you to change or adjust your walk with Him? What changes have you already made, and how are they affecting your relationship to God?

_____

_____

_____

_____

• **Your marriage**
What changes have you felt were important to make in your marriage as a result of this study? What changes have you already made, and how have they helped your relationship?

_____

_____

_____

_____

• Your family

What sorts of things has God challenged you to handle differently with your children or others in your family? How will these changes affect your relationship with them?

_____

_____

_____

_____

• Your relationship with others

What adjustments do you feel God is asking you to make in your schedule in order to make more time for others in your life? What changes have you made, if any? What has been the result?

_____

_____

_____

_____

• The management of your home

What changes do you feel God is leading you to make in how you keep your family and home environment running smoothly? If you have already made changes, what are they, and how have they made a difference in your everyday lives?

_____

_____

_____

_____

• Your employment

Are there any changes or adjustments you feel you should make regarding your job? Should you work less hours, or at least more family-friendly ones? How about getting a job with more flexibility, trying not to bring your work home with you, or even quitting your job? What has worked for your family so far?

_____

_____

_____

_____

• Overcoming past and present obstacles

If there have been any obstacles you've overcome, or dealt with successfully during the course of this study, what has helped you do so? Are there still some areas on which God wants you to work? If so, what are they, and what is God asking you to do?

_____

_____

_____

_____

• Serving with your gifts

Do you have a special gifting, or is there an area of service, in which God has challenged you to step out and use for His glory? How have you prepared to use your gifts or stepped out in this area of ministry so far?

_____

_____

_____

_____

• Reaching out to the lost

Have you sensed God breaking your heart for the lost? If so, what has impacted you, and what efforts have you made to share Christ with those around you?

_____

_____

_____

_____

CHANGE COMES ONLY THROUGH HIS STRENGTH

If you've attempted to make substantial changes in any of these areas, you have likely been reminded of what I've said many times already: *We can't do the work of the Spirit in the strength of the flesh!* Let's remind ourselves of the method the Scriptures give us to bring about change and produce fruit in our lives.

Read John 15:1–11.

What foundational statement can be found in verse 5?

_____

_____

According to verses 4, 5, and 8, what progression takes place in the amount of fruit God wants to produce in our lives?

_____

_____

According to these verses, what is the key to producing this fruit, as well as the key to "abiding" in Christ found in verse 10?

_____

_____

If there's anything that I truly hope you will take away from this study it's that God has appointed you to bear fruit for Him, and that you can only do so through _loving God_ and _loving other people._ We must attempt to balance the "loves" of our lives so that we can be free to do all that He desires. In the process, we loose ourselves from the stranglehold of the world's system, letting go of some things and taking hold of God's priorities.

Many people without balance go like gangbusters for God, but forget the part about doing it _in love!_ Others think that if they're just "nice people" that should be good enough, but they never get anything productive done! We're called to do _both_ — love God with our whole hearts, _and_ love our neighbors — those people whom God brings into our world — as ourselves. And the only way we can do this is to be directed and empowered by the Holy Spirit on a daily basis.

Read John 14:10, 16–17.

According to verse 10, where did Jesus get the power to both do His work and keep His life balanced?

_____

_____

_____

_____

Where is the best place we can get counsel about how to do this in our own lives?

_____

_____

THE COST OF DISCIPLESHIP

Rick Warren has this to say about discipleship:

> Sadly, a quick review of many popular Christian books reveals that many believers have abandoned living for God's great purposes and settled for personal fulfillment and emotional stability. That is narcissism, not discipleship. Jesus did not die on the cross just so we could live comfortable, well-adjusted lives. His purpose is far deeper: He wants to make us like himself before he takes us to heaven. This is our greatest privilege, our immediate responsibility, and our ultimate destiny.[1]

Read Mark 8:34–35.
According to verse 34, there are three steps to becoming a disciple of Christ. List these steps, and explain what each one means to you.

1._____

2._____

3._____

What does it mean to lose your life for Christ's sake?

_____

_____

_____

We must deny ourselves, take up our cross, and then follow Jesus. Denying what we want and preferring what Christ wants, we allow Him to be the Lord of our decisions. In other words, when our will and His will contradict each other, we choose His will, abandoning all that He doesn't want for us, and embracing all that He does. Jesus was our example in this when He prayed, _Not my will, but yours be done_ (Luke 22:42). Then we choose to follow, listening intently for His voice, reading His Word, and allowing Him to lead us.

The incredible paradox is that in losing our lives, we actually find them! And when that happens, we finally figure out who we are, and why we're here. That's God's promise. We trade our old sinful lives for new ones, full of joy, purpose, direction, and eternal rewards to come. *He heals our past, empowers our present, and directs our future!* Best of all, we enter an eternal relationship with the Lover of our souls.

COME AWAY, MY BELOVED

Friend, don't ever forget how much you're loved! You're God's unique creation, His one-of-a-kind masterpiece. He sees you as beautiful and without blemish through the blood of His Son. You're the apple of His eye, and your friendship with Him was worth the death of His Son. There is no greater love on earth than the love we can experience through a meaningful relationship with our Creator.

Who in their right mind would resist this kind of love? And yet so often, we stay too busy to spend time with Him, or we allow our relationship to grow stale through our neglect or disobedience. What are we thinking?! What could possibly be worth more to us than a thriving love relationship with Someone who loved us enough to die for us? *God invites us to come away with Him to a place of rest, refreshment, direction, and intimacy every single day.* That's where we receive the power we need to walk the walk.

Read Mark 6:26–31.
What kind of day had the apostles had? Why?

_____

_____

What did Jesus suggest they do to be refreshed, and what can we learn from this when we have "one of those days" ourselves?

_____

_____

_____

Jesus' words in that passage sound very similar to those found in Matthew 11:28: *"Come to me, all you who are weary and burdened, and I will give you rest."* When you're tired and frustrated, remember His words, "Come to Me." When you're lonely or depressed, He says, "Come to Me." When life doesn't make sense, and you're at the end of your rope, He says, "Come to Me." And when you're on top of the world and your heart is bursting with joy, He still says, "Come to Me."

I have to admit, I've made practically every mistake known to man, and even come up with some of my own! I've been guilty way too many times of choosing busy over best and the quick fix over the longer, life-changing times with God. I've leaned toward the world's mindset, and then like a fisherman reels in a fish on a hook, I've had to reel my heart and mind back to subjection to Christ. Like I said, I've blown it so many times I could write (and am writing) a book about it!

Yet, through many trials and much error, I've learned that my time spent with God in prayer and reading His Word are truly the treasures of my life. Nothing in my life even comes close to my relationship with God. He's the pearl of great price that's worth selling all I have to call mine. Is He yours?

REFRESHMENT OR RITUAL?

God's invitation to intimacy never changes, and His line is never busy! When we quiet our hearts and sit at His feet, we find strength and direction for each day. But that will never happen if we zip in and zip out of our quiet time in record time, just so we can check it off our list! There's no refreshment there. When we get away from simply coming to God to worship Him and seek His face, our quiet time becomes nothing more than another demand on our time. *We exchange a refreshing relationship for a repetitious ritual.* In other words, it becomes a rut. How tragic!

In the same way, we can't afford to get our "revelation from God" secondhand, trying to live off of the spiritual experience of someone else. No matter who that someone is, or how spiritual they may be, they can't be our only source in determining God's will. We must hear that from God for ourselves.

God wants to *know* you, and for you to know Him. Remember that in Matthew 7:22–23, Jesus said, *"Many will say to me on that day, 'Lord, Lord, did we not prophesy in your name, and in your name drive out demons and perform many miracles?' Then I will tell them plainly, 'I never knew you. Away from me, you evildoers!'"* Our whole walk with Christ is about that all-important relationship. That's why there are no shortcuts to spiritual maturity. It only comes from *knowing Christ!* Why? Because He is our very Source of life!

When we come into God's presence, the room becomes a sanctuary — a sacred refuge from the craziness of the world around us. That's where we find that *peace of God, which transcends all understanding* (Philippians 4:7). His peace is supernatural, and His promises are true. We will truly experience this peace *only* when He's in charge.

ENJOY THE RIDE!

When God is at the helm of our ship, we can lean back and enjoy the ride! He's in control. We can breathe easier knowing He's the Almighty, and we don't have to be! We don't have to stress about anything; instead, we pray. We make sure we're using our time as He desires, and then we trust Him to work out the things that concern us. Easier said than done? Let's look at three principles that can help us make this our daily practice.

Read each of the following scripture passages, and list the principle you find in each that can guide you toward prayer and away from stress. Begin each answer with the words, "I don't have to live under stress because . . . "

1. Ephesians 3:20

_____

_____

_____

2. Philippians 4:6–7

_____

_____

_____

3. Romans 8:28

_____

_____

_____

Author Jennifer Rothschild writes:

> I once saw a bumper sticker that said, "God is my co-pilot." That sounds spiritual, but it isn't true. The truth is that on our faith journey, God is the Pilot, and we must follow, not co-lead. We are not in charge of the journey. We are called to restfully follow. Our Pilot is completely trustworthy. There's no need for us to fret, for He is capable of navigating us through all the turbulence of the journey. We can rest in the very situation where He has lovingly placed us. And when we do, we'll find the fabulous freedom of following.[2]

ONE SHOT TO MAKE A DIFFERENCE

Read John 9:4.

Explain what this verse means to you. What "work" is God calling you to do?

_____

_____

_____

Do you remember that "roller coaster of Extreme Faith" I talked about earlier? Well, I'm in the front seat with my hands up! That's what makes this life exciting. I'm trying to *work... while it is day* (John 9:4 KJV) — while I have the opportunity to make a difference for all of eternity! We only have one shot in this life because when the buzzer goes off, the game is over, and I want to score all the heavenly "points" I can while there's still time on the clock!

Of course, "scoring points" requires obedience. Without it, God won't give us bigger and more exciting ventures in faith, because we haven't proven ourselves to be trustworthy. It's when we obey with our whole hearts that our walk with God becomes exciting and fulfilling. I don't know about you, but I don't want to miss a single thing God has for me, even if it means some scary situations and some difficult battles. I'd rather end my life with some battle scars, than have sat and watched the entire game on the sidelines!

As God speaks to our hearts about doing new things, we must always remember that He never expects us to do His work in our ability or resources alone. We must continue to live in *His* strength and with *His* resources. *We do the natural part, and He does the supernatural!* We work hard to prepare — to study, learn, pray, and practice — and He anoints us, flows through us, opens doors for us, and gives us the supernatural ability we need to get from point A to point B.

That's what it means to be "co-laborers" with Christ. We don't show up like lazy slobs to be Christ's ambassadors. We must give our best and do all as unto the Lord (see 1 Corinthians 10:31 and Colossians 3:17). He meets us where our ability ends, and we move into His strength. He provides the tools and opportunities for us to fulfill His purposes.

STEPPING OUT OF THE ARK

When God calls us to "pick up our hammers" and join Him in His work, it often requires us to take big steps of faith. Let's put ourselves in Noah's shoes for a moment. He did what he knew to do in the natural, and then God did the rest in the supernatural.

Read Genesis 6:13–22 and 7:13–16.
Have you ever questioned God's judgment when you didn't know all the details? What was the result?

_____

_____

_____

_____

How can you go beyond your own "mixed-up" feelings and obey what God tells you to do despite how things look in the natural?

_____

_____

_____

When God told Noah to build the ark, it had been a long time since they'd had a real downpour. As a matter of fact, it had never rained before! *Noah didn't know what rain was, let alone a flood.* And yet God knew that building the ark was Noah's only chance for survival. When God asks us to do something that doesn't make sense to us, often we try to "straighten Him out," don't we? How crazy is that? The great omnipotent Creator of the universe surely knows what is going on better than we ever would.

Meanwhile back at the ranch, Noah was faced with a monumental task. He was stepping out purely in faith that he had heard from God. So he found a tree, worked on it all day, and by sundown he'd made his first board. Can you imagine? Year after year Noah worked on this massive "thing," with friends and neighbors mocking him as he diligently tried to lead them to God. *They must have thought he'd gone off the deep end, when they were the ones who were about to find themselves in deep water!*

One-hundred-and-twenty long years later, Noah nailed that last nail. He put down his hammer with his blistered hands, reached for a Gatorade, and found a shade tree where he could rest his tired back. As he stared at the gigantic structure in front of him, he must have wondered if he was *absolutely sure* he'd heard from God. By this time the people around town had decided he was a lunatic. He'd invested his entire life in this project. *He'd done all he could possibly do in the natural, and now it was up to God to make sense of it.*

But just as he started to wonder if he really was crazy after all, an amazing thing happened. While he watched, a tiger came wandering up, and then another, and they walked up the ramp and right into the ark! Noah must have sat up with interest. Then a beautiful little lamb emerged from the woods with its partner, and they followed the tigers up the ramp. Normally they would have made a tasty lamb-chop lunch for tigers, but not today! Two by two every species of wild animal came out of nowhere, and without once trying to munch on the lower parts of the food chain, they calmly entered the ark!

In amazement, Noah and his family watched this fascinating event, and word got out around town, too. Soon a nervous crowd gathered to see this miracle, as the almighty God confirmed Noah's words by validating his years of hard work before them. As the wind began to pick up, and the clouds began to darken, so did their hopes of survival. If what Noah had warned them of was true, they were in big trouble.

Finally, like the final punctuation mark at the end of an exciting story, when Noah's family and all the animals were aboard ship, *God closed the door,* closing them in in safety, and closing the world out to reap the consequences of their sin. And the rest is history. *Noah wasn't crazy — he was faithful, and he will reap eternal rewards for his faith in God.*

It's one thing to read about this kind of faith, but it's another thing to experience it. God probably won't call us to build another ark, but He will definitely call us to step out of the boat! Like Noah, when we've heard from God, we will be called to do all we can possibly do in our abilities, and then let God make sense of the rest.

Not that we step out without confirming our sense of direction in the Word. We never want to do anything "weird" in the name of faith, or get off into extra-biblical activities that aren't from God. But with that in mind, let me encourage you — *don't miss your chance!* Climb onto that roller coaster of Extreme Faith, buckle up, and let God take you on the ride of a lifetime!

BUILDING GOD'S KINGDOM

Read 1 Peter 2:4–6.

What does it mean to be a "living stone, " or to be built into a "spiritual house?"

_____

_____

What promise is given in verse 6 that applies to us as we sign up for God's construction crew?

_____

_____

Let's take a look at another quote from Rick Warren's book, *The Purpose Driven Life:*

> It's not about you. The purpose of your life is far greater than your own personal fulfillment, your peace of mind, or even your happiness. It's far greater than your family, your career, or even your wildest dreams and ambitions. If you want to know why you were placed on this planet, you must begin with God. You were born *by* his purpose and *for* his purpose.[3]

One of those purposes is to further God's kingdom. Think of it this way: You wouldn't hire a carpenter to build a house for you if he didn't have any tools. To be effective, he would need to learn the trade, become skilled in his profession, and bring whatever tools he had with him. In the same way, we must study the Word of God, offer our gifts and skills to Him, and then go to work building His kingdom. He provides the blueprint, the crew, the materials, and His own craftsmanship. We simply bring whatever gifts and skills we have — and a heart that's willing to learn from the Master.

When we do this, the most amazing thing happens! God begins to use our gifts to build His kingdom. Meanwhile, next door He's using another believer's skills to build his little piece of the kingdom, and down the block He's doing the same thing — until He's built a whole neighborhood! In a nearby city, the same thing is happening, and in the next town down the road, until He is building His kingdom across the country and throughout the world.

The important thing to remember as we throw our hearts into what God wants us to do is to strive to maintain balance. *Building God's kingdom always starts at home.* We should not make time for everyone but our families, even though that's an easy pattern in which to get entangled. Instead, we lay a biblical foundation in each of our children's hearts, and build up our husbands and family members through each hug, every prayer, each act of tough love and gentle kindness. One day at a time, one moment at a time, we choose to lay down our own lives and take the time to build them up in God's love.

As we do this, we'll be investing in something that will outlast us, like a deposit from our account to theirs. Yet in God's economy, investing in the lives of others has a boomerang effect. We give and give, and yet our accounts are never empty. He keeps filling them up with joy, peace, love, and all the resources we need to continue giving generously. We can't lose when we do it God's way!

Read Proverbs 11:25 and Luke 6:38.
How do these scripture passages relate to this principle of investing our lives into others?

_____

_____

What are some practical ways we can do this at home, and away from home?

_____

_____

_____

Applying our faith and employing our gifts to serve others, as it tells us to do in 1 Peter 4:10, is also part of being on God's crew. We say "yes" to the Spirit, and "no" to the flesh, being careful to nurture that intimate relationship with our heavenly Father. *Eliminating the things that distract us, we make time to concentrate on the specific things God has called us to do.* Through God's strength we overcome obstacles that would otherwise paralyze us with fear or take us off track, and we submit them to God. Finally, after guarding time for our husbands and families, we find the place God has designed for us to serve, and *go for it* with all our heart, soul, mind, and strength!

THE ABUNDANT LIFE IS A BALANCED LIFE

This is the abundant life that the Scriptures speak of. It's also the balanced Christian life that will be rewarded when at long last we meet our Savior face to face. How rewarding it would be to hear Him say, "Well done, my good and faithful servant. Enter into Your Master's happiness!" (see Matthew 25:21). Let's live for that moment, organizing each day and capturing each moment in preparation for that all-important meeting. Whatever the cost — we will have all of eternity to enjoy the rewards we've sent on ahead of us!

This became crystal clear to me the other night as I tucked our youngest daughter, Anna, in bed. As we read a few pages in Bruce Wilkinson's book, *A Life God Rewards (For Girls Only),* these words seemed to hold special meaning for me: "Just for a moment, think about this world as **here** and think about heaven as **there**. Now then, remember these words: *What we will have **there** will depend on what we do with what we have **here**.*"[4]

This principle is found throughout Scripture.

Read Matthew 6:19–21, 33.
What daily changes do you need to make in order to truly place living for God as the focus of your life?

_____

_____

_____

Now take a few moments to sum up one thing that you've learned throughout the weeks of this study that has helped you as you "seek first God's kingdom." How has it changed you and your outlook on how you spend your time?

_____

_____

_____

_____

As history winds down, there's never been a more exciting time to live for God. Yes, the battles rage around us, and we get tired and beat up once in a while. But when all is said and done, our lives will boil down to what we've done to honor God. The tests we go through here are just preparation for the final exam in heaven when our works will be "tested" by fire. But the good news is that we can use our "Book," and the Holy Spirit is here to help us find the answers!

There's an old adage I try to live by that says, "Only one life, 'twill soon be past, Only what's done for Christ will last." When our works are born out of a growing relationship with our heavenly Father, and we guard our time with Him like a treasure, our lives will bring glory to His name. We can walk in the peace that passes understanding, and function from a place of tranquility in God's presence, regardless of our circumstances. When we do, our lives will become focused and fruitful, and we will flourish as the women God has designed us to be!

PRAYER

Dear Lord, as I come to the end of this study, once again I surrender all to You. Have Your way in my life, Lord. Help me to be the wife, mom, and woman You want me to be. Help my life to be focused on accomplishing Your will, and let the joy of the Lord truly be my strength. I love You, Lord, and I thank You for all You've done for me. In Christ's name I pray. Amen.

SUMMARY POINTS

• True balance comes only as we focus on the Cross.
• We can move forward as we rest in Christ's completed work on the Cross.
• Change comes only through His strength.
• God invites us to join Him in building His eternal kingdom.

From Print to Power: Personal Application

1. Take some time this week to flip through the pages at the end of each chapter. List some of the things you've felt God directing you to do, adding any further direction you feel you've received this week.

_____

_____

_____

_____

2. Now, using a few key words from each, separate these various directives into two lists:

THINGS I'M DOING	THINGS I'M NOT DOING
_____	_____
_____	_____
_____	_____
_____	_____
_____	_____
_____	_____
_____	

3. Pray about each one, asking God to give you specific ideas about how to integrate these things into your routine, and *when* He wants you to pursue them. Likewise, pray about what God wants you to eliminate from your routine. Think about scheduling changes you may need to make in order to do what He asks of you.

4. Take some time to write a love letter to God, thanking Him for all He's done for you already and what He has planned for your future.

NOTES

CHAPTER ONE

[1]Rick Warren, *The Purpose Driven Life* (Grand Rapids: Zondervan, 2002), 17.

CHAPTER TWO

[1]This definition was gleaned from the *New American Standard Exhaustive Concordance.* Three Greek words were consulted: *pronoeo, pro,* and *noeo.*

[2]Warren, 21.

CHAPTER THREE

[1]Mark Balmer, "There's a Miracle in Your Home, Part 2." Sermon delivered 11/16/02 at Calvary Chapel, Melbourne, FL.

CHAPTER FOUR

[1]John Palmer, "Be All You Can Be in '90." Sermon delivered 1/10/90 at First Assembly of God Church, Des Moines, IA.

[2]Ibid.

[3]Ibid.

[4]Ibid.

CHAPTER FIVE

[1]Darlene Wilkinson, *The Prayer of Jabez for Women* (Sisters, OR: Multnomah, 2002), 40.

[2]Mark Balmer, "Be Ready to Do God's Will." Sermon delivered 8/16/03 at Calvary Chapel, Melbourne, FL.

CHAPTER SIX

[1]D. L. Moody, quoted in Cynthia Heald, *Becoming a Woman of Excellence* (Colorado Springs, CO: NavPress, 1986), 34.

CHAPTER EIGHT

[1]Bruce Wilkinson, "A Biblical Portrait of Marriage," videotape series (Walk Through the Bible Ministries, 1995).

[2]Balmer, "There's a Miracle, Part 2."

[3]Mark Balmer, "There's a Miracle in Your Home, Part 3." Sermon delivered 11/12/02 at Calvary Chapel, Melbourne, FL.

[4]Balmer, "There's a Miracle, Part 2."

[5]Marilyn Long, "On the Path to Oneness." Bible study teaching delivered 1/31/90 at First Assembly of God Church, Des Moines, IA.

[6]Willard F. Harley, Jr., *His Needs, Her Needs* (Grand Rapids: Fleming H. Revell, 2000), 12–13.

CHAPTER NINE

[1]Ted Tripp, *Shepherding a Child's Heart* (Wapwallopen, PA: Shepherd Press, 1995), 54.

[2]Ibid., xvii–xviii.

[3]Mark Balmer, "Esther." Sermon delivered 10/16/02 at Calvary Chapel, Melbourne, FL.

[4]Tripp, 48.

CHAPTER TEN

[1]Henry Blackaby and Claude V. King, *Experiencing God* (Nashville: Lifeway, 1990), 25.

[2]Mark Balmer, "Handling Storms on the Sea of Life." Sermon delivered 1/11/04 at Calvary Chapel, Melbourne, FL.

[3]Mark Balmer, "Job: The Focus of Satan's Attack." Sermon delivered 1/7/03 at Calvary Chapel, Melbourne, FL.

[4]Mark Balmer, "Solomon's Wise Choice." Sermon delivered 6/19/01 at Calvary Chapel, Melbourne, FL.

[5]Mark Balmer, "For Such a Time As This." Sermon delivered 10/22/02 at Calvary Chapel, Melbourne, FL.

CHAPTER ELEVEN

[1]Blackaby and King, 65.

[2]Ibid., 67.

[3]Ibid., 68.

[4]Warren Wiersbe, *On Being a Servant of God* (Grand Rapids: Baker, 1999), 5.

[5]Ibid., 8.

[6]Jim and Karen Covell and Victoria Michaels, *How to Talk About Jesus Without Freaking Out* (Sisters, OR: Multnomah, 2000), 31.

[7]Ibid., 88.

CHAPTER TWELVE

[1]Warren, 177–178.

[2]Jennifer Rothschild, *Lessons I Learned in the Dark* (Sisters, OR: Multnomah, 2002), 162.

[3]Warren, 17.

[4]Bruce Wilkinson, *A Life God Rewards (For Girls Only)* (Sisters, OR: Multnomah, 2002), 71.

Real People... Real Life... Real Problems... Real Answers...
THE INDISPUTABLE POWER OF BIBLE STUDY

Through the Bible in One Year
Alan B. Stringfellow • ISBN 1-56322-014-8

God's Great & Precious Promises
Connie Witter • ISBN 1-56322-063-6

Preparing for Marriage God's Way
Wayne Mack • ISBN 1-56322-019-9

Becoming the Noble Woman
Anita Young • ISBN 1-56322-020-2

Women in the Bible — Examples To Live By
Sylvia Charles • ISBN 1-56322-021-0

Pathways to Spiritual Understanding
Richard Powers • ISBN 1-56322-023-7

Christian Discipleship
Steven Collins • ISBN 1-56322-022-9

Couples in the Bible — Examples To Live By
Sylvia Charles • ISBN 1-56322-062-8

Men in the Bible — Examples To Live By
Don Charles • ISBN 1-56322-067-9

7 Steps to Bible Skills
Dorothy Hellstern • ISBN 1-56322-029-6

Great Characters of the Bible
Alan B. Stringfellow • ISBN 1-56322-046-6

Great Truths of the Bible
Alan B. Stringfellow • ISBN 1-56322-047-4

The Trust
Steve Roll • ISBN 1-56322-075-X

Because of Jesus
Connie Witter • ISBN 1-56322-077-6

The Quest
Dorothy Hellstern • ISBN 1-56322-078-4

God's Solutions to Life's Problems
Wayne Mack & Joshua Mack • ISBN 1-56322-079-2

A Hard Choice
Dr. Jesús Cruz Correa • Dr. Doris Colón Santiago
ISBN 1-56322-080-6

11 Reasons Families Succeed
Richard & Rita Tate • ISBN 1-56322-081-4

The Fear Factor
Wayne Mack & Joshua Mack • ISBN 1-56322-082-2

Embracing Grace
Judy Baker • ISBN 1-56322-083-0

Courageous Faith
Keith Bower • ISBN 1-56322-085-7

5 Steps to Financial Freedom — Workbook
James D. Wise • ISBN 1-56322-084-9

5 Steps to Financial Freedom — Clothbound
James D. Wise • ISBN 1-56322-091-1

Forged in the Fire — Shaped by the Master
Tim Burns • ISBN 1-56322-086-5

7 Keys to Hearing God's Voice
Craig von Buseck • ISBN 1-56322-087-3

Balance at the Speed of Life — Workbook
Barb Folkerts • ISBN 1-56322-088-1

Balance at the Speed of Life — Clothbound
Barb Folkerts • ISBN 1-56322-092-X

Journey to Jesus
Florence Littauer with Marita Littauer • ISBN 1-56322-089-X

WE WANT TO KNOW
WHAT YOU THINK
ABOUT THIS
BIBLE STUDY!

Please send any comments
or suggestions to:

HENSLEY PUBLISHING
6116 East 32nd Street
Tulsa, Oklahoma 74135
www.hensleypublishing.com